Corporate Social Responsibility

Over the last 30 years, c　　　　　　　　ssponsibility (CSR) has become a household term, reflecting a combination of factors that we have come to associate with that most catch-all of terms "globalization," including the widespread popular concern with such social issues as the environment and international human rights.

Corporate Social Responsibility examines the history of the idea of business ethics (which goes back at least to ancient Mesopotamia), before exploring the state of CSR today. This book argues that only a broad-gauged understanding of the purpose of business as creating value for its community of stakeholders can generate a sustainable future. The book suggests that corporations still have a long way to go, but remains optimistic. The book's sanguine interpretation of the current state of corporate affairs and a recommended way forward results not only from the author's analysis, but also his direct experience. This book presents the case that we are in the midst of a major paradigm shift in our understanding of the purpose of business and that this new understanding holds much promise for business being a significant force for a more just and peaceful world.

This work provides a concise overview of CSR and an important examination of the present and future work of the United Nations Global Compact and will be of interest to students of international organizations, international business and corporate social responsibility.

Oliver F. Williams is a member of the faculty of the Mendoza School of Business at the University of Notre Dame and is the director of the Center for Ethics and Religious Values in Business.

Routledge Global Institutions Series

Edited by Thomas G. Weiss
The CUNY Graduate Center, New York, USA
and Rorden Wilkinson
University of Manchester, UK

About the series

The Global Institutions Series has two "streams." Those with blue covers offer comprehensive, accessible, and informative guides to the history, structure, and activities of key international organizations, and introductions to topics of key importance in contemporary global governance. Recognized experts use a similar structure to address the general purpose and rationale for specific organizations along with historical developments, membership, structure, decision-making procedures, key functions, and an annotated bibliography and guide to electronic sources. Those with red covers consist of research monographs and edited collections that advance knowledge about one aspect of global governance; they reflect a wide variety of intellectual orientations, theoretical persuasions, and methodological approaches. Together the two streams provide a coherent and complementary portrait of the problems, prospects, and possibilities confronting global institutions today.

The most recent titles in the series are:

Reducing Armed Violence with NGO Governance (2013)
edited by Rodney Bruce Hall

Transformations in Trade Politics (2013)
by Silke Trommer

Committing to the Court (2013)
by Yvonne M. Dutton

Global Institutions of Religion (2013)
by Katherine Marshall

Crisis of Global Sustainability (2013)
by Tapio Kanninen

Corporate Social Responsibility

The role of business in
sustainable development

Oliver F. Williams

Routledge
Taylor & Francis Group

LONDON AND NEW YORK

First published 2014
by Routledge
2 Park Square, Milton Park, Abingdon, Oxon OX14 4RN

and by Routledge
711 Third Avenue, New York, NY 10017

Routledge is an imprint of the Taylor & Francis Group, an informa business

British Library Cataloguing in Publication Data
A catalogue record for this book is available from the British Library

Library of Congress Cataloging in Publication Data
Williams, Oliver F.
Corporate social responsibility : the role of business in sustainable development / Oliver F. Williams. – 1 Edition.
    pages cm. – (Routledge global institutions series ; 79)
Includes bibliographical references and index.
    1. Social responsibility of business. I. Title.
    HD60.W545 2013
    658.4'08–dc23
            2013018914

ISBN: 978-0-415-82496-5 (hbk)
ISBN: 978-0-415-82497-2 (pbk)
ISBN: 978-0-203-74675-2 (ebk)

Typeset in Times New Roman
by Taylor & Francis Books

Contents

Foreword by the series editors

The current volume is the seventy-ninth title in a dynamic series on global institutions. These books provide readers with definitive guides to the most visible aspects of what many of us know as "global governance." Remarkable as it may seem, there exist relatively few books that offer in-depth treatments of prominent global bodies, processes, and associated issues, much less an entire series of concise and complementary volumes. Those that do exist are either out of date, inaccessible to the non-specialist reader, or seek to develop a specialized understanding of particular aspects of an institution or process rather than offer an overall account of its functioning and situate it within the increasingly dense global institutional network. Likewise, existing books have often been written in highly technical language or have been crafted "in-house" and are notoriously self-serving and narrow.

The advent of electronic media has undoubtedly helped research and teaching by making data and primary documents of international organizations more widely available, but it has complicated matters as well. The growing reliance on the Internet and other electronic methods of finding information about key international organizations and processes has served, ironically, to limit the educational and analytical materials to which most readers have ready access—namely, books. Public relations documents, raw data, and loosely refereed websites do not make for intelligent analysis. Official publications compete with a vast amount of electronically available information, much of which is suspect because of its ideological or self-promoting slant. Paradoxically, a growing range of purportedly independent websites offering analyses of the activities of particular organizations has emerged, but one inadvertent consequence has been to frustrate access to basic, authoritative, readable, critical, and well-researched texts. The market for such has actually been reduced by the ready availability of varying quality electronic materials.

For those of us who teach, research, and operate in the area, such access to information and analyses has been frustrating. We were delighted several years ago when Routledge saw the value of a series that bucks this trend and provides key reference points to the most significant global institutions and issues. They were betting that serious students and professionals would want serious analyses, and they were right. We have assembled a first-rate team of authors to address that market, and the titles—in print and electronic form—are selling well. Our intention remains to provide one-stop shopping for all readers—students (both undergraduate and postgraduate), negotiators, diplomats, practitioners from nongovernmental and intergovernmental organizations, and interested parties alike—seeking insights into the most prominent institutional aspects of global governance.

Corporate Social Responsibility

Over the last 30 years, corporate social responsibility (CSR) has become a household term, reflecting a combination of factors that we have come to associate with that most catch-all of terms "globalization," including the widespread popular concern with such social issues as the environment and international human rights. Perceptions of corporate behavior are a crucial component of a company's public profile—important to investors and consumers alike. Corporations are increasingly viewed as having responsibilities not just to their shareholders but also to "stakeholders." This term used to refer to a relatively narrow group—employees, customers, and suppliers in addition to shareholders—but is now broadly perceived as including the wider community at large.

Corporate Social Responsibility examines the history of the idea of business ethics (which goes back at least to ancient Mesopotamia) before exploring the state of CSR today. Oliver Williams argues that only a broad-gauged understanding of the purpose of business as creating value for its community of stakeholders can generate a sustainable future. The book suggests that corporations still have a long way to go, but he remains optimistic. His sanguine interpretation of the current state of corporate affairs and a recommended way forward results not only from his analysis but also his direct exposure to two companies (Merck and Homeplus) that provide elements of "learning" and perhaps even can serve as a model. This book is the third in this series that deals in some way with the role of transnational corporations. The first two were *The World Economic Forum* and *The International Organization for Standardization*, and the fourth is a forthcoming volume on the *UN Global Compact*.[1]

A business-ethics consultant and Holy Cross priest as well as professor at the Business School of the University of Notre Dame, Ollie Williams is one of the world's leading experts on corporate social responsibility. He began his career in South Africa in the 1980s, about which he wrote *The Apartheid Crisis*, which advocated for divestment as a justifiable ethical and business stance in the face of white-minority rule.[2] Since then he has written 14 books and numerous articles on business ethics, in addition to teaching in the United States, South Africa, and Asia. He has also served on the board of directors for the United Nations Global Compact (UNGC) Foundation since 2006.

We are pleased to publish this book on such an underexplored subject in the series. It fills a significant gap in the literature by providing a clear and insightful introduction to the social role of business and its relationship to international affairs. We wholeheartedly recommend it and, as always, welcome comments from our readers.

Thomas G. Weiss
The CUNY Graduate Center, New York, USA
Rorden Wilkinson
University of Manchester, UK
May 2013

Notes

1 Geoffrey Allen Pigman, *The World Economic Forum: A Multi-stakeholder Approach to Global Governance* (London: Routledge, 2007); Craig N. Murphy and JoAnne Yates, *International Organization for Standardization: Global Governance Through Voluntary Consensus* (London: Routledge, 2009); and Catia Gregoratti, *UN Global Compact* (London: Routledge, forthcoming 2014).
2 Oliver F. Williams, *The Apartheid Crisis: How We Can Do Justice in a Land of Violence* (San Francisco, Cal.: Harper & Row, 1986). His more recent titles include: *Economic Imperatives and Ethical Values in Global Business: The South African Experience and Global Codes Today*, co-authored with S. Prakash Sethi (Notre Dame, Ind.: University of Notre Dame Press, 2001), and the edited volume *Peace Through Commerce: Responsible Corporate Citizenship and the UN Global Compact* (Notre Dame, Ind.: University of Notre Dame Press, 2008).

Foreword

The role of business in society is no longer just the subject of public debates but has become an issue in board rooms of corporations around the world. Just a decade ago, corporate responsibility was synonymous with philanthropy. Debates were typically confined within ideological paradigms where public and private spheres were clearly defined, and classic views on shareholder responsibility were dominant within the business and investor communities. At the corporate level, communication and marketing departments were in charge, and corporate social responsibility, or "CSR," lacked strategic or operational dimensions.

Fast forward to 2013: corporate leaders around the world have put sustainability on their agendas, recognizing the growing relevance and urgency of global environmental, social and economic challenges. They see how sustainability issues affect the bottom line and thus are looking beyond traditional business and financial factors. The fact is that sustaining growth and leadership is associated with the ability to navigate these issues. More and more companies are taking action; over 7,000 companies in 140 countries have joined the UN Global Compact and adopted a principles-based management and operations approach. Importantly, the investment community is increasingly considering the materiality of sustainability, more often considering factors such as sound environmental stewardship, social responsibility and good ethics in calculating a company's long-term value.

What accounts for this fundamental transformation, and where can this journey lead us?

First, companies have gone global. They no longer can take shelter behind the relative predictability of national consensus on business-society questions where they are headquartered. As companies have gone East and South, following the migration of economic growth, they have built global value chains and invested in new markets. This has brought with it rapid diffusion of know-how and helped hundreds of millions of people to escape abject poverty while ensuring growth. However, it has also exposed corporations to risks that must be managed, often without drawing on government support.

Global companies today are faced with extreme poverty, unacceptable working conditions, and environmental degradation in their backyard, and are more often operating in markets where corruption is systemic and violence a daily occurrence. In such situations corporations have a choice to make. They can either uphold high standards—based on universal principles—or they can muddle through. Large domestic companies in emerging and developing markets face similar choices. For these companies, corporate sustainability and responsibility has immediate material relevance. It can mean the difference between costly damage to growth prospects or the opportunity to build long-term investments and markets.

Second, the rapid diffusion of communication technologies and the empowerment of people through access to information have two fundamental implications for corporate responsibility. Hiding missteps or negative fall-out from investments and operations—no matter how deep down the supply chain—is no longer an option. Transparency, including significant improvements in disclosure on social, environmental and governance issues, has become a necessary tool for management and societal engagement. In addition, information accessibility and the spread of social networks on the internet have challenged traditional forms of authority. Earning a license to operate increasingly requires public legitimacy, and this can only be earned through proactive engagement on the topics that move societies. The ascendancy of the stakeholder concept over the past decade is a testimonial to this important development.

Third, as technology and market interdependencies connect people and nations ever more closely, debates about values and morals have become important again. As corporations search for globally applicable benchmarks, the decades of work by the UN can play an obvious and important role. This is where the UN Global Compact, and the "power of the principles" provide a unique value—as the initiative's Ten Principles are derived from universally accepted frameworks on human rights, labor, environment, and anti-corruption to which all governments have agreed. Having a reference point is a helpful first step, but the real challenge comes when principles are tested in challenging environments. By joining together with like-minded corporations either at the global level or through the 101 Global Compact country networks, businesses are learning how to advance and partner on issues and dilemmas, with an array of innovative collaboration models emerging.

Fourth, traditional boundaries between public and private goods have become fuzzy in a globalized world. As power and responsibility go hand in hand, business is expected to do more in areas that used to be the exclusive domain of the public sector—ranging from health and education, to community investment and environmental stewardship. As planetary boundaries put an ever-greater premium on natural goods such as air, water and biodiversity, fundamental questions of valuation and accounting are bound to gain relevance—further blurring definitions and challenging old concepts. The search for new boundaries that define responsibilities of the private sector is taking place in many forums, and varies greatly from country to country. This search will intensify and further stimulate the corporate sustainability agenda.

When the Global Compact was launched in 2000, few companies were exploring the notion of sustainable business and the long-term impacts of their operations on the environment and society. Today, there are thousands of companies advancing corporate sustainability through a number of global initiatives.

Much progress has been made to attune business toward more responsible practices, yet there is still a long way to go until companies everywhere put principles into practice. As the world's largest corporate sustainability movement, the Global Compact's business participants represent just a sliver of the world's estimated 80,000 multinationals and millions of smaller enterprises. A quantum leap is needed. This will require moving beyond incremental actions to widespread impact. Increasing the scale and intensity of sustainability work globally will involve reaching companies that have yet to embrace the agenda, motivating less-advanced companies to deepen their efforts, and spurring front runners to lead the way to the next generation of sustainability performance.

The challenge now is to make corporate sustainability a transformative force in achieving a better world—a world defined by peace, inclusiveness, opportunity and environmental sustainability. *Corporate Social Responsibility* offers a creative discussion of where we have been and how we might move forward in the future.

Georg Kell
Executive Director, UN Global Compact
New York, May 2013

Acknowledgments

Tracing the history of corporate social responsibility (CSR) has been a most rewarding project not only because CSR is crucial for a healthy planet today but also because the account traces my own intellectual journey. Reflecting on that journey, I am reminded of the many people to whom I owe a debt of gratitude and will discuss several of those here.

I joined the field teaching business ethics and business in society in the early 1980s and in 1985 I published a book on apartheid in South Africa. Subsequently I served on the board of directors of the Sullivan Principles. I came to know the Reverend Leon Sullivan (1922–2001), the civil rights leader and charismatic pastor of a major black church in Philadelphia. Sullivan was a passionate advocate of civil and political rights for blacks in South Africa and the first black man on the board of directors of General Motors. Watching Sullivan, I saw a person who stood for what he believed to be right, even in the face of much opposition. He had a strong moral compass that affected all who worked with him and I am grateful for his leadership.

During the apartheid years I also served on the board of directors of the United States-South Africa Leadership Development Program (USSA-LEP), a nongovernmental organization (NGO) funded by foundations and businesses that brought talented black students from South Africa to the United States for education. In that capacity I met many top business leaders and could see that most were not ready publicly to oppose apartheid and take steps to dismantle it. One lesson I learned here is that often business does not speak with one voice. Jim Burke (1925–2012), the then CEO of Johnson & Johnson, stands out as one of those prophetic leaders with a deep moral sense. I recall his words that apartheid was morally wrong and that no matter what the cost to the company, J&J would have to oppose it. I am grateful for Burke's influence on my thinking.

In 2006 I was appointed to the three-person board of directors of the United Nations Global Compact Foundation (UNGC). The UNGC is the world's largest voluntary corporate citizenship initiative, with over 7,000 businesses committed to advancing human rights, enhancing the environment, and overcoming corruption. In a 2012 meeting with business leaders from China, I asked one CEO how he approached the UNGC principle on human rights in a country that is often criticized on that score. He assured me that he was full of hope that someday, in the not too distant future, China would be a leader in that regard: "We are working on it, give us time." I am grateful to him and other business leaders of his kind who give us hope for a healthy future.

This book adapts some of my earlier writings on South Africa and the UN Global Compact and I am grateful to the University of Notre Dame Press, Roman & Littlefield Publishers, and *The Business Ethics Quarterly* for permission.

I offer my thanks to a number of people who have assisted me in this project, especially my assistant at the Center for Ethics and Religious Values in Business at the University of Notre Dame, Deb Coch. The manuscript would still be on yellow notepads if it were not for the talented staff of the Faculty Support Center at Notre Dame and I am especially indebted to Tamara Chapman-Springer and Diana Stauffer. The dean of the Mendoza College of Business at Notre Dame, Roger Huang, generously approved my leave for the 2012–13 academic year and I am most grateful. I also appreciate his breadth of understanding and support for educating business students who will create sustainable value for all stakeholders.

The book was written in Seoul, South Korea, where in the 2012–13 academic year I was an "International Scholar" and visiting professor at Kyung Hee University. Teaching in the School of Management and lecturing widely in the community was a joy. The Korean people are hard-working, good natured and fun to be with. I am grateful to the university for giving me the time and space for this project. My graduate assistant at KHU, Andrew Hyun Jong Oh, provided invaluable assistance and I thank him. I am especially grateful to Stephen Yong-Seung Park, professor of human resource management and dean of the Office of International Affairs at Kyung Hee. Stephen was not only my faculty sponsor but also a good friend who taught me much about Asia.

Georg Kell, the executive director of the UN Global Compact since its founding in 2000, graciously agreed to write a foreword and I am most grateful. Finally, while I have drawn on the work of many scholars and colleagues in writing this book, I alone am responsible for any errors in the factual presentation or interpretation.

Oliver F. Williams, C.S.C., University of Notre Dame, USA
Kyung Hee University, Seoul, Korea
July 2013

Abbreviations

ACHAP	African Comprehensive HIV/AIDS Partnership
ACOA	American Committee on Africa
AMCHAM	American Chamber of Commerce
ARV	antiretroviral
CED	Committee for Economic Development
CEO	chief executive officer
COP	Communication on Progress
COSATU	Congress of South African Trade Unions
CSR	corporate social responsibility
CSV	creating shared value
ECOSOC	UN Economic and Social Council
ESG	environmental, social/ethical and governance issues
EU	European Union
FCPA	Foreign Corrupt Practices Act
GE	General Electric
GM	General Motors
GRI	Global Reporting Initiative
GSK	GlaxoSmithKline
ICCR	Interfaith Center on Corporate Responsibility
ILO	International Labour Organization
IRRC	Investor Responsibility Research Center
KMAC	Korean Management Association Consulting
MDGs	Millennium Development Goals
MOU	memorandum of understanding
NAACP	National Association for the Advancement of Colored People
NGO	nongovernmental organization
OAS	Organization of American States
OECD	Organisation for Economic Co-operation and Development

OHCHR	Office of the UN High Commissioner for Human Rights
PRI	Principles for Responsible Investment
PRME	Principles for Responsible Management Education
R&D	research and development
SACC	South African Council of Churches
SASAC	State Assets Supervision and Administration Commission
SDGs	Sustainable Development Goals
SRSG	special representative of the UN secretary-general
TBL	triple bottom line
TI	Transparency International
UN	United Nations
UNCTC	United Nations Commission on Transnational Corporations
UNDP	United Nations Development Programme
UNEP	United Nations Environment Programme
UNGC	United Nations Global Compact
UNIDO	United Nations Industrial Development Organization
UNODC	United Nations Office on Drugs and Crime
USSALEP	United States-South African Leadership Development Program
WCC	World Council of Churches
WEF	World Economic Forum
WTO	World Trade Organization

Introduction

What is the role of business in society: To do well and to do good? These seemingly contradictory aspirations appear to be deeply rooted in the human species and have always had a special urgency for many involved in business. This book presents the case that we are in the midst of a major paradigm shift in our understanding of the purpose of business and that this new understanding holds much promise for business being a significant force for a more just and peaceful world. Examples of what business leaders are saying and what their companies are doing and why they are doing it will be provided. What we are seeing according to its proponents is the emergence of a view of the firm as a socially responsible political actor in the global economy and as an institution that can generate not only material wealth but also wealth that nourishes the full range of human needs, what some call spiritual capital. Needless to say, this view is not without its critics and that perspective will be presented as well.

Neoclassical economics asserted a strict division of labor between the private and public sectors. Governments are charged to provide public goods and deal with the challenges of social justice, while collecting taxes to pay for these services. If the people are not pleased with the way elected politicians establish priorities and mediate interests, they can vote them out of office. Business, on the other hand, has another task: to produce goods and services at a reasonable price while returning on investment. Business has made tremendous progress not only in the quantity of goods and services available but also in the quality of life. Technology that enables us to enjoy good music, medicines that increase life expectancy and decrease infant mortality, and machinery that humanizes work, are only a few of the fruits of capitalism.

The strict division of labor between the private and public sectors is no longer a reality in our time. Under the rubric of corporate social responsibility (CSR), corporate citizenship, or sustainability, companies are taking increasing responsibility for problems in the wider society. At least in practice, there is clearly a change in progress in the way the responsibilities of the private and public sectors are apportioned. Many argue for a wider role for the purpose of business than simply making profit: that the purpose of business is not simply to make a profit, but rather that business is a community of persons and that this community can foster development of society as well as people.

Chapter 1 discusses the emergence of corporate social responsibility, its history and development. The idea that business ought to be concerned about social and environmental issues is as old as business itself. Scholars report that 5,000 years ago the business of logging elicited concern about the forests and laws were in place to protect them. King Hammurabi in Mesopotamia, around 1700 BC, enacted laws that exacted the death penalty for those whose business was responsible for the death of a person.[1] This chapter will largely focus on the last 60 years, as this is the period when CSR as an academic discipline and as a mainstream activity of business emerged. The case of the role of business in the struggle to overcome apartheid is examined in some detail as it illustrates the changing role of business in society.

Chapter 2 focuses on how a discussion of the purpose of business advanced the cause of CSR and how the South African experience gave business leaders a new perspective. CSR was often rejected by scholars and business leaders alike but it finally came to be embraced by almost all involved. Andrew Carnegie's life (1835–1919) perhaps embodied the tension involved in trying to do well in business and at the same time realize his social ideals of advancing the least advantaged. He finally resolved the tension by dividing his life into two periods, first making a huge amount of money, often ruthlessly, and then retiring from business and becoming a generous philanthropist.[2] Milton Friedman, the Nobel Prize economist, provided the theoretical underpinnings for those who would follow Carnegie: business should "make as much money as possible while conforming to the basic rules of the society ... "[3] In recent years society's expectations of business have changed and people have employed both hard and soft law, the political process as well as the power of nongovernmental organizations (NGOs), to change the ground rules of business. Today there is a newly emerging understanding of the purpose of business and CSR is widely accepted by many citizens, scholars and business leaders.

Chapter 3 asks what the best driver is for CSR, and how we can enlist more companies to participate in the quest for a sustainable future. Should CSR only be embraced when it pays? What if there is no apparent business case to be made for a CSR initiative? Should a company do it and, if so, why? Should a company be legally obliged to get involved in CSR activity? Morally obliged? The chapter suggests that an understanding of the purpose of business as the creation of sustainable value for all stakeholders is the best hope for forward movement to a sustainable future.

Chapter 4 focuses on the United Nations Global Compact (UNGC) as the most effective way to garner the critical mass of companies needed to overcome global poverty and establish global norms for multinational business. Most scholars and business leaders familiar with the globalization of business acknowledge the need for some coordinating body to facilitate cooperation and convene meetings. I argue that the UN Global Compact with its global reach and respected presence best serves this role.[4]

Chapter 5 concludes that the changing role of business is well underway and that business leaders should get involved in the ongoing dialogue about the purpose of business. In 1959, Harold R. Bowen in his *Social Responsibilities of the Businessman* asked the question with which we are still grappling today: "What responsibilities to society may businessmen reasonably be expected to assume?"[5] It is this question that will occupy us for some time in the future. It is in the best interests of business and society that all major stakeholders be involved in this discussion.

Given the problems of our time, the Global Compact has advanced a vision that has a critical mass of companies moving from incremental progress to transformational action to advance sustainable development. To have an idea of what companies might do to participate in this vision, examples of two model companies are presented: Merck, a US-based, large multinational pharmaceutical company; and Homeplus, a medium-size leader in the retail business in South Korea.

Finally, the chapter concludes with a reminder that although business, as the key driver of economic activity, has a primary role in advancing sustainable development, the movement will never succeed without active participation of all the actors, including governments, NGOs, consumers, educators, investors, suppliers and workers.

Notes

1 Januarius J. Asongu, "The History of Corporate Social Responsibility," *Journal of Business and Public Policy* 1, no. 2 (2007): 1–18.
2 Andrew Carnegie, *Autobiography of Andrew Carnegie* (Middlesex: The Echo Library, 1923).
3 See Milton Friedman, "The Social Responsibility of Business is to Increase its Profits," *New York Times Magazine*, 13 September 1970: 32–33, 122, 124, 126.

4 Oliver F. Williams, "The UN Global Compact: The Challenge and the Promise," *Business Ethics Quarterly* 14, no. 4 (2004): 755–74. See also Oliver F. Williams, ed., *Peace Through Commerce: Responsible Corporate Citizenship and the Ideals of the United Nations Global Compact* (Notre Dame, Ind.: University of Notre Dame Press, 2008).
5 Harold R. Bowen, *Social Responsibilities of the Businessman* (New York, NY: Harper and Row, 1953), 11.

1 Corporate social responsibility

Its history and development

- **The challenge: reconciling and integrating economic and social values**
- **Some theoretical foundations: academics and practitioners**
- **Living between the times: tracing of a paradigm shift with the case study of South Africa**
- **Conclusion**

Corporate social responsibility, or CSR, as a new field of management studies began to emerge in the early 1950s and took on added importance in the 1990s. While CSR is a difficult concept to define precisely, generally it is thought to be that behavior of business which seeks to solve social problems in the wider society that would not ordinarily be addressed in the pursuit of profits. Seeking public goods is generally the goal of CSR activities by business. The underlying sentiments of CSR, to make a profit while enhancing the quality of life, especially for the least advantaged, have often been present in business people. Andreas Georg Scherer and Guido Palazzo capture the complexity of CSR when they call it an "umbrella term" and include within it all the discussions about the role and responsibilities of business in society whether they are in the fields of business ethics, stakeholder theory or business and society.[1] As will become clear throughout the volume, I argue that, at root, CSR is concerned with the very purpose of business.

By examining how entrepreneurs struggled with the challenge of integrating economic and social values in the context of changing expectations of society, this chapter presents how CSR developed. The chapter opens by focusing on the challenge of integrating and reconciling economic and social values. Then some important contributions of scholars and practitioners are discussed. The major part of the chapter discusses a case study of how business addressed the apartheid issue in South Africa and how that case illuminates a paradigm shift that was underway, a new understanding of the role of business in society. Finally the conclusion of the chapter summarizes some of the things learnt from this period.

The challenge: reconciling and integrating economic and social values

Today the hallmark of CSR is not how money is spent but how money is made. There have been some important business leaders in the past who had noble sentiments but they found it impossible to reconcile their concern for social and human values with their drive for significant financial success. For example, Andrew Carnegie, in the midst of a strikingly successful career as far as financial success goes, had many second thoughts about whether he was really successful. In his words: "To continue much longer overwhelmed by business cares, and with most of my thoughts wholly upon to make more money in the shortest of time, must degrade me beyond hope of permanent recovery."[2] Carnegie finally resolved the tension by retiring from business and dedicating his life to philanthropy.

CSR says it is possible to manage a very successful business and resolve the tension between economic and social values not by compartmentaliza-tion, as Andrew Carnegie did, but rather by integrating the values into the strategic plan of a business. It may be helpful to cite an example which will illustrate that the trajectory of CSR these last 70 years has yielded some remarkable theory and practice. Consider the case of John Mackey, CEO of Whole Foods, an US$8 billion company with over 300 stores specializing in natural foods. For Mackey, the purpose of business is not to make money but to create sustainable value for all stakeholders— employees, customers, suppliers, the environment, the wider society, and yes, of course, the shareholders. Mackey has co-authored a book to explain his philosophy, *Conscious Capitalism*.[3] Other major business leaders are also following a new business paradigm. Bill Gates, founder of Microsoft, speaks of "creative capitalism."[4] Ben and Jerry, founders of the Vermont ice cream company, speak of "caring capitalism."[5]

Some theoretical foundations: academics and practitioners

While the struggle to resolve the tension between human/social and economic/financial values has had a long history, the first scholar to articulate clearly what was at stake was Howard Rothman Bowen (1908–89). In his important 1953 book *Social Responsibilities of the Businessman* (apparently there were no women in the field at that time), Bowen's major contribution is that he perceived earlier than most that business leaders ought to be striving to make the values of business congruent with the values of society.[6] Because of the power of large businesses, there was a corresponding responsibility to care for society. Just how much responsibility business ought to assume was an open question for Bowen. Author of 14 books, Bowen had a PhD in economics and did postdoctoral work in Cambridge, UK and the London School of Economics. He served as dean of the College of Commerce at the University of Illinois from 1947 to 1952, and later went on to assume a number of leadership positions in higher education, including Grinnell College, the University of Iowa, and Claremont Graduate University. Another pioneer in the field was Theodore Kreps (1897–1981), who anticipated the current discussion of the triple bottom line reporting with his writings on the "social audit." A Stanford University professor, Kreps argued that an audit should measure a firm's progress against some standard social responsibility criteria. His course at Stanford, first taught in 1931, anticipated many of the topics discussed today in a class on CSR.

Morrell Heald (1945–2004), a professor of American Studies at Case Institute of Technology, profiles the activities of business in the CSR area from 1900 to 1960. He highlights a question that continues to occupy scholars: are there any limits to voluntary action and what is the role of government in CSR? His *Social Responsibilities of Business* first published in 1970 recounts what companies have done under the CSR rubric in the first 60 years of the twentieth century. His book was reissued in 1988 under the title *The Social Responsibilities of Business: Company and Community, 1900–1960.*[7]

Much of the insight presented by these early scholars reflecting on the role of business in society was a result of observing what leading business leaders were actually doing. Typically top business leaders are intelligent and charismatic entrepreneurs who demonstrate creative and innovative strategies to meet the challenges of the times. They are not particularly adept at developing new concepts and theories to account for what they are doing. One notable exception in this regard was Frank W. Abrams, a talented leader who rose through the ranks of Standard Oil of New Jersey (called Exxon today) to eventually become its chairman of the board of directors. While Abrams does not claim to have fully molded Standard Oil in accord with his creative ideas, he clearly was a forerunner in formulating a vision and purpose for business in the twenty-first century. In a 1951 article in the *Harvard Business Review*, Abrams advanced a number of germinal ideas that have only come to fruition in recent years, and some are not fully developed yet.[8] Abrams, without benefit of the many concepts and theories that management takes for granted today, was 50 years ahead of his time in discussing crucial issues for business. Some of these include: the purpose of business; education for business leaders; corporate citizenship; the license to operate; the creation of value for all stakeholders; the fundamental role of trust; CSR; and sustainability. It may be helpful to see what Abrams wrote in 1951.

- *The purpose of business.* " ... business management in the United States is acquiring more and more the characteristics of a profession ... Professional men do not work solely for themselves, but also for the good of mankind ... the serving of individual objectives by identifying them with the common good ... will lead to the increasing recognition of business management as a profession—for such is the essence of a profession."
- *The education of business leaders.* "Because a large and well-established enterprise is accustomed to looking far into the future and making long-term decisions, it particularly needs broad social and political understanding as well as economic understanding."
- *Corporate citizenship.* "Management, as a good citizen, and because it cannot properly function in an acrimonious and contentious atmosphere, has the positive duty to work for peaceful relations and understanding among men ... "
- *The license to operate.* "Public approval is no less essential to the continual existence of today's kind of business than adequate capital, or efficient management."
- *The purpose of business: the creation of value for stakeholders.* "The job of professional management ... is to conduct the affairs of the enterprise in its charge in such a way as to maintain an equitable and workable balance among the claims of the various directly interested groups: the stockholders, employees, customers, and the public at large."
- *Trust.* "But all the advertising space we can buy, exhorting others to believe in us as businessmen, will go unheeded, and all our speeches and statements will fall on deaf ears, until folks believe that we understand and are concerned with their problems."
- *CSR.* "Business managers must merit the confidence of the nation, so that they can more effectively contribute to the solution of the many complex social questions of our time."
- *Sustainability.* " ... in the long run the public interest corresponds with the basic interests of their individual businesses."

Later chapters in this book will show the present state of the development of the CSR concept and it will be apparent just how prophetic Abrams was in his 1951 article. Following Abrams there were several scholars who published landmark studies in CSR, including Benjamin M. Selekman (1959),[9] Richard Eells (1956),[10] William Frederick (1960),[11] Keith Davis (1960),[12] Joseph McGuire (1963),[13] and Clarence Walton (1967).[14] Frederick's work will be discussed later but a few words on the contributions of Davis and Walton may be helpful.

Keith Davis, one of the important pioneers in the field of CSR, formulated what he called the Iron Law of Responsibility.[15] His point was that in the long run those who have power and do not use it in a way that society considers responsible will lose that power. If an organization has social power it should also have social responsibility. If an organization wants to keep its reputation for being ethical, it should voluntarily take on some of the problems of the wider society in which it operates. In the past it was enough for a large corporation to produce good products at a fair price, while following the law and ethical customs. This was sufficient for a company to be perceived as legitimate by the public, but today corporations seem to be victims of their own success. They have become so efficient, competent, and therefore wealthy and powerful, that people expect them to lend some of their time, talent and resources to social projects, sacrificing a certain amount of profit to assist the wider society. The size issue is clearly dominant here since the economic power of individual multinationals is often greater than many of the 190 nation-states in the world.

Clarence Walton, an academic who served as a dean of Columbia Business School as well as a university president, wrote an important book in 1967 titled *Corporate Social Responsibilities*. In it he advanced the idea that a corporation is really as much "a social and political entity as an economic unit." His observation of business, especially big business, was that it "is consciously placing public interest on a level with self-interest and possibly above it." He noted that enlightened business was voluntarily supporting higher education, the arts, inner-city projects, job training, civil rights, and environmental issues. Much of his discussion anticipated what was later widely proclaimed as corporate citizenship or sustainability. Walton certainly did not speak for the majority of the business community of his time but he did outline a vision for the future.

Many of Walton's ideas were echoed in a 1971 document *Social Responsibilities of Business Corporations* issued by the Committee for Economic Development (CED).[16] In many ways this was a remarkable turn of events, as the CED is a major business organization of 200 senior-level executives and the document endorsed CSR, noting that there was a changing social contract between business and society. The document outlined a three-tiered framework for CSR: an inner circle concerned with the economic function (products, jobs, and economic growth); an intermediate circle concerned with meeting the new social values while carrying forward the economic function (environmental issues, human resource issues, and customer expectation issues); and the outer circle concerning ways that business should engage in activities improving the social environment in the wider society (for example, overcoming poverty and inner-city problems).

While the CED is not the spokesperson for the business philosophy, it is a significant business coalition that commands attention. The 1971 CED document is clearly committed to social responsibility and is largely based on enlightened self-interest: that for business to thrive, society must thrive. The late 1960s brought a new kind of activism—civil rights, consumer, anti-war, environmental, anti-poverty, and so on. The fear was that if business did not respond, surely government would. The 1971 document advanced the idea that the corporation was becoming a socio-economic organization under the terms of a new social contract with society.

Lest one think that the 1971 CED document settled the issue of the new role of business in society, one had only to wait until 1979 when the CED issued a new paper with a decidedly different philosophy. Titled *Redefining Government's Role in the Market System*, the document reverted to the traditional position that market efficiency was the best way to achieve social progress.[17] The nonmarket orientation of the 1971 document, the social responsibility dimension, was not in evidence in the 1979 statement. Rather than suspending the movement for a broader role of business in society, however, the 1979 document was, in my view, simply a reminder that the march toward a fully developed concept of CSR was still a work in progress. The two documents from the CED, 1971 and 1979, gave ample evidence that there was not a consensus among business leaders about how advances in society are best accomplished.

Living between the times: tracing of a paradigm shift with the case study of South Africa

What the two differing CED documents reveal was that business was in the midst of a major paradigm shift. In 1971 George Steiner wrote approvingly about CSR and later developed an important distinction which sheds light on the differences in the documents.[18] His "market capitalism" model was describing the way business had been done in the past and, to some extent, in the present. The responsibility of business is largely restricted to producing goods and services while returning well on investment. His "business ecology" model was a new model and a work in progress: the social contract between business and society requires responsiveness by business to ethical issues in the external environment.[19] Those business leaders signing off on the 1979 document had the world view of the market capitalism model and believed that the social and economic advancement of society are best enabled by market efficiency. Those arguing for the 1971 CED statement had the world view of the business ecology model and, without doubting the value of market efficiency, believed that some social advancements are best enabled by business directly solving problems in the wider society. As we shall see, the second model won out but not without much struggle. It may be helpful to track the paradigm shift in some detail by following the case of the companies in South Africa as they made efforts to overcome apartheid.[20]

In discussing the issue of South Africa and dismantling apartheid with managers of major businesses in the United States, one common theme that emerges is almost a disbelief that, in fact, the pressures became so great that almost 150 US companies decided to leave the country between 1985 and early 1990. These pressures were largely orchestrated by the church groups and associated anti-apartheid organizations that had begun that struggle in the 1970s. In one way or another the "hassle factor" reached a threshold where, for many companies, it made little sense to stay. Quoting Xerox Chairman David T. Kearns, discussing the 1987 Xerox disinvestment, the *Wall Street Journal* captured the sentiment of many top managers: "It was clear things were continuing to deteriorate on all fronts," he said. The nation's economy and social climate were worsening, pro-disinvestment groups' criticism was rising, and Xerox was beginning to lose sales in the United States to local governments that were banning contracts with companies doing business in South Africa.[21]

Although disagreeing over the means of dismantling apartheid, almost all Americans believed apartheid was wrong. Apartheid in South Africa was controlled by over 300 racial laws denying blacks the rights many people of the world take for granted—the right to vote, to move freely within the country, to attend decent schools, and to have the opportunity to live in suitable housing. Focusing on human rights, concern about these racist policies on the part of US groups dates back to 1912 when the National Association for the Advancement of Colored People (NAACP) provided assistance to what later became the Africa National Congress of South Africa. The momentum only began, however, in 1953 with the founding of the American Committee on Africa (ACOA) by the white US Methodist minister George Houser. Under Houser, the ACOA campaigned for total US disinvestment from South Africa.

In 1957 the ACOA sponsored a Declaration of Conscience campaign with the "World-Wide Day of Protest" that featured Eleanor Roosevelt and Martin Luther King, Jr. For the most part, the ACOA campaign of the 1950s did not attract much interest in the United States.

In Houser's view, it was the media attention given to official violence against blacks in South Africa that especially caught the attention of Americans.[22] On 21 March 1960, a demonstration against the pass laws in Sharpeville resulted in the police killing 67 and wounding 180 people. Later in 1976, 15,000 school children demonstrating in Soweto were fired upon by security forces. Finally, unrest and violence throughout the country between 1984 and 1987 added to the ever-growing American interest groups supporting total disinvestment.

Defining the situation: business as part of the problem from the activist perspective

To be sure, the television and other media coverage of these tragic events brought the apartheid problem into the living rooms of middle America, but does it explain the ever expanding pressure for total disinvestment? Houser and others think not and focus instead on the fact that business, at least until 1984, was perceived as being too cozy with the white government in South Africa and relatively unconcerned with the plight of the majority of the people who suffered under apartheid.

What was the proper role of business in advancing the civil and political rights of blacks in South Africa? While from the 1950s to early 1970s business leaders made no concerted efforts to determine a consensus response, church groups were busy formulating their answer. In the 1950s Methodist minister George Houser was fashioning an action-oriented organization (ACOA) that was destined to be most influential. It was not until the middle to late 1960s, however, that college students, civil rights leaders, and church groups began to devise strategies in response to the evil of apartheid. In 1975, building on work begun in the 1960s by ACOA, a major offensive was launched by church groups coordinated by the ICCR (the Interfaith Center on Corporate Responsibility)—a large coalition of Protestant denominations and an ad hoc group of Catholic dioceses and religious orders, housed in the New York City headquarters of the National Council of Churches—against bank loans to the Republic of South Africa. Forty-seven banks, including some of the major banking institutions in the United States, were threatened with a mass withdrawal of deposits and continued shareholder pressure unless loans to the Republic of South Africa ceased. Although initially the campaign did not have a significant effect on the loan policy of the banks, it did give much visibility to the apartheid problem. Tim Smith, executive director of the ICCR, reflecting on the discussions with bank officials, noted that he observed a major shift in the thinking of managers.

Initially, as the ICCR and its religious investors challenged managers to take responsibility for supporting the evils of apartheid with their bank loans, the managers responded that their sole responsibility was to find reliable businesses that would return on investment (the market capitalism model). As the campaign progressed, however, Smith observed a gradual opening on the managers' part to hear and act upon the social and moral concerns of the church groups. Business came to realize that what was at stake was the very legitimacy of business in the minds of some important constituencies and that it was in the interest of business to interact with those forces impinging on the business system.

What was happening here was a gradual paradigm shift from the market-capitalism model to the business-ecology model.[23] While it was never clear to the interest groups whether the banks were acting on principle or protecting self-interest, after mounting enormous public pressure, the religious coalition was finally successful in terminating all loans. To be sure, this process took over 10 years. Were the bank managers actually convinced that they, as bank officers, had an ethical obligation to advance the human rights of the South African blacks or did they simply capitulate in the face of overwhelming public opinion in the United States? At least two banks (Chemical and Chase Manhattan) did state their opposition to apartheid as the reason for ending loans. Did they have an adequate model to conceptualize the ethical issues in the context of a business environment? Probably not.

The shareholder resolution campaign developed into a major avenue of mobilizing public pressure on business. In 1971 the first shareholder resolution ever to come to a vote called for the termination of General Motors' (GM) operations in the Republic of South Africa and was presented by the Episcopal Church. (By 1990 over 500 shareholder resolutions had been presented to over 90 companies with operations in South Africa.) Although the resolution in 1971 garnered only 1.29 percent of the votes, it was a watershed event in that it was the occasion for the Reverend Leon Sullivan, a new member of the board of GM, to call for the withdrawal of GM and all US business from South Africa until apartheid was dismantled. While Sullivan clearly did not carry the day at the GM board meeting, he did make a very significant point: that human rights concerns were the province of the board and that he would not rest until that notion was accepted. According to Sullivan, in 1971 most of the board of GM or any other company were not prepared to consider factoring human rights considerations into business decisions. As will be discussed later, by 1991 this broader agenda for business had become almost standard practice for a growing number of companies. This study hopes to shed light on that transition in thinking.

While Sullivan was unable to persuade the GM board to take a stand in 1971, he continued to mull over the various options to overcome apartheid in South Africa. There was a growing expectation in the United States that business should be involved in social issues, and advocacy groups, encouraged by the success of Ralph Nader's initiatives, began to grow in importance. What gave rise to this rather sudden increase in nonmarket forces or interest-group activism? One of the most formative experiences that may have set the tone for activism in the United States was the civil rights movement of the 1960s. The many who participated in this event, actively or passively, came to feel a new power to transform society. Evil did not have to be tolerated; unjust social structures could be changed with strategy and persistence. In my view, the antiwar movement, the rise of local community organizations, and the experience of the civil rights movement and its use of the media and creation of heroes provided the model and the power that brought the current activist movements to birth.

At the same time, several other important developments have provided fertile soil for the growth of the activist movements. During the last 30 years the media has achieved significant power to shape public opinion on social issues, and informed public opinion has led to financial and other support for a wide variety of organizations championing social issues. In addition, the two major political parties were the vehicles that carried the concerns of the people through the public-policy process, but they no longer function effectively in the eyes of many people; today's interest groups perform many of the roles that were abdicated by the political parties. That US business should avoid racist policies in South Africa has had an especially compelling claim on Americans because of their own, often unsuccessful, experience in trying to overcome a racist past.

It was in this climate that the Reverend Sullivan, acting independently of the ICCR affiliates, invited the top executives of 15 of the largest US corporations with operations in South Africa to attend a meeting to discuss the means of overcoming apartheid. Held on 29 January 1976, at Sands Point, Long Island, an IBM facility, the meeting focused on Sullivan's agenda: either the companies use their power to overcome apartheid or they leave South Africa. It is important to note that Sullivan was making a justice argument here. He was not arguing that multinational companies operating in South Africa ought to advance human rights based on charity or virtue but rather that companies in South Africa had a moral obligation to fight for the human rights because they are so essential to living a life with dignity. While all the business leaders involved may not have agreed with Sullivan's philosophy, there was a preliminary agreement at the meeting to seek a consensus on a set of principles that would guide all US businesses in South Africa in a common task of dismantling apartheid.

It was not until over a year later and after much compromise that, on 1 March 1977, Sullivan was able to announce that 12 of the companies had found consensus on six principles. The companies were American Cyanamid, Caltex Petroleum, Citicorp, Ford Motor, IBM, International Harvester, Minnesota Mining and Manufacturing, Mobile Oil, Otis Elevator, Union Carbide, Burroughs, and General Motors. The original principles, listed below, did not touch on seeking civil and political rights but focused only on employment practices in the workplace. The original principles called for:

- nonsegregation of the races in all eating, comfort, and work facilities;
- equal and fair employment practices for all employees;
- equal pay for all employees doing equal or comparable work for the same period of time and minimum wages well above the minimum living level;
- initiation of and development of training programs that will prepare, in substantial numbers, Africans and other blacks for supervisory, administrative, clerical and technical jobs;
- increasing the number of Africans and other blacks in management and supervisory positions; and
- improving the quality of employees' lives outside the work environment in such areas as housing, transportation, schooling, recreation and health facilities.

Sullivan struggled during 1976 to persuade the companies to use their power to pressure the South African government to dismantle the apartheid laws and grant all full civil and political rights, but he was not successful. He finally settled for the original six principles. While Sullivan was hoping to bring the companies into compliance with the emerging social contract for business, stressing civil and political rights, what is sometimes called "bridging," the business leaders prevailed so that the final version of the 1977 principles was more of a buffering strategy;[24] that is, they were an attempt to influence the social contract so that it would be less intrusive on business. The principles, while meeting some of the concerns for human rights, were largely seen by advocacy groups as an ineffective attempt to influence the emerging social contract and avoid overwhelming pressures for complete disinvestment. In terms of strategic response patterns,[25] from the activist point of view, the companies were involved in "domain defense" while seeming to accede to domain expansion; that is, they were preserving their position in South Africa by responding to some of the concerns of those who threatened to undermine their legitimacy. The principles may have been perceived partly as an attempt to co-opt those activist groups that were championing complete disinvestment and replace them by the Reverend Sullivan and the principles program (Domain Offense— Encroachment). To be sure, Sullivan is and was thought by activist leaders to be an honorable man with great charisma and deep convictions about the dignity of all people. His 1977 Principles for US business in South Africa, however, appeared to the activist interest groups to divert attention from the real issues rather than help in the struggle for political rights. The ICCR led the opposition. While in retrospect, it is clear that in 1977 the companies had a golden opportunity to forge a new alliance with the coalition of religious groups under the umbrella of the ICCR, because they chose not to include political rights in the principles, the new initiative did not have a prayer. Timothy Smith, executive director of the ICCR, promptly issued the coalition response in a public statement:

> Is the "Statement of Principles" a case of offering a stone when a child asks for a fish? The issue in South Africa at this time is black political power; it is not slightly higher wages or better benefits or training programs, unless these lead to basic social change. As one South African church leader put it, "These principles attempt to polish my chains and make them more comfortable. I want to cut my chains and cast them away."[26]

George Houser, the executive director of the ACOA, wrote a letter to the Reverend Leon Sullivan shortly after the principles were issued, severely criticizing them. Sullivan responded, indicating that he, too, was less than satisfied with the principles but hinting that he had plans to amplify them:

> The Statement of Principles you received represents only a "first step" in an attempt to see if American-based companies operating in the Republic of South Africa can be a significant influence for change in getting rid of apartheid as a system and totally unacceptable way of life. The ultimate objective of my effort is to assist in the ending of apartheid, the ending of the oppression and destruction

of human life that has already reached unendurable, inhumane, and savage proportions.[27]

Sullivan, in a 1977 letter to the director of the National Council of Churches of Christ in the United States, Robert C.S. Powell, explicitly states his ultimate goal to have the companies aggressively oppose the government: "Further, it is our aim to have all companies participate in intensive lobbying efforts to let the South African government know that participating American businesses want to see all industrial discriminatory laws changed, and want to see an end to oppression and terrorism, and want to see an end to the apartheid system."[28]

Lest anyone have any doubts that the Sullivan Principles were not sufficient to meet the concerns of many activist leaders, 26 US officials representing a number of Catholic organizations and most major mainline Protestant denominations, coordinated by the ICCR, issued a letter to corporations in South Africa indicating their position:

> We call on all US corporations investing in South Africa to adopt a policy to cease any expansion and begin to terminate present operations in the Republic of South Africa unless and until the South African government has committed itself to ending apartheid and has taken meaningful steps toward the achievement of full political, legal and social rights for the black majority.[29]

From the perspective of 2013, there would be good cause to wonder why the 12 CEOs who agreed upon the original principles in 1977 did not include a strong statement on the need to seek political rights for blacks aggressively, even if such a campaign would violate South African law. Even a statement indicating that the companies would reassess remaining in South Africa if some movement on political rights did not transpire would have been acceptable to many. Most in the United States thought this was the moral thing to do. Furthermore, such a move would have pleased some in the large coalition of church groups and may have drawn business and at least some of the church groups together in common cause. This, of course, was the original intention of Reverend Sullivan, and it was the strategy that ethicists and most commentators counseled. Seven years later, in 1985, under enormous pressure from religious groups, Sullivan finally insisted on adding opposition to government apartheid policies to the principles; even then there was still strong opposition from the business community. An editorial in the *New Republic* captures the dilemma that seems to have troubled many in the business community:

The Reverend Leon Sullivan wants to add to his principles a requirement that companies lobby politically for free movement of labor—that is, for the end of pass laws, and so on. But even some of Sullivan's staunchest corporate backers are resisting the notion of political involvement. Yet this goes to the essence of the claim that capitalism and apartheid are incompatible. Companies that profit from investment in South Africa are morally implicated in that nation's political system. If they wish to discharge that moral burden with the assertion that they're helping to change the system, they have to be ready to prove it. Otherwise, they should get out.[30]

To understand the resistance of the business community, one has to realize that such business involvement in political affairs was considered out of the question in the market capitalism model. Several comments from business leaders in 1977 may illustrate the adamantine resistance. For example, Henry Ford II, chairman of the board of Ford Motor Company, wrote to Leon Sullivan on 11 November 1977: "We are making good progress in implementing the Statement of Principles agreed to earlier this year ... *As a businessman, I don't know what more the US companies can or should do in South Africa* to try to solve a problem which is political, social and moral, as well as economic, in nature."[31]

Again, in a letter to Sullivan, dated 1 November 1976, R.H. Herzog, chairman of the board and chief executive officer of 3M, said: "To the degree that South African law and South African government policy allows, our subsidiary there has taken aggressive action to conform to these principles."[32]

Finally, the Conference Board had a meeting in South Africa on 15 March 1987, in New York City, which six US companies attended, most of which were signers of the principles. Although no formal minutes "were allowed to be taken," the informal notes of Sal G. Marzullo of the Mobil Corporation, retained in the archives of Temple University, report as follows:

It was agreed business cannot do more than improve the conditions of its workers. We cannot transform the nature of South African society and we will have serious problems with South Africa if we try, but we must do all that we can as quickly as we can to improve the social and economic well-being of all of our black and other non-white employees.[33]

Because of the omission of political rights concerns, the coalition of religious groups opposing apartheid not only did not perceive the Sullivan

Principles as helping to enable democratic change, but they found them subversive to the cause of liberation, and thus they continued to press for the complete disinvestment of all US firms. Elizabeth Schmidt, a prominent activist, was most critical and adopted a cynical response in her work on the principles, *Decoding Corporate Camouflage: US Business Support for Apartheid*.[34] In a 1982 address to the State of Connecticut's Task Force on South African Investment Policy, Schmidt quotes Bishop Tutu who gives a capsule summary of the key issue: "Our rejection of the code is on the basis that it does not aim at changing structures. The Sullivan Principles are designed to be ameliorative. We do not want apartheid to be made more comfortable. We want it to be dismantled."[35]

A new way for business to integrate economic and social values: forged under social pressure

Between 1977 and 1982 enormous pressures were brought to bear on US corporations to leave South Africa. Shareholder resolutions continued as did university and college divestment initiatives. In 1982 the pressure tactics took a new turn when three state legislatures (Connecticut, Michigan, and Massachusetts) passed bills restricting investment of state funds (pension funds, endowments, etc.) in companies and banks with business connections in South Africa. This was only the beginning of a powerful trend, much of which was a response to the "constructive engagement" of the Reagan Administration that eased many of the existing federal government restraints.

It was in this climate that Sullivan was able to persuade the companies, now over 90 signatories, to be even more aggressive in seeking black equality. Three amplifications were added to the principles prior to 1982. In addition to the six principles, companies must:

- acknowledge the rights of Africans to form and belong to trade unions, whether registered with the government or not;
- support changes in South Africa's influx-control laws to provide for the right of African migrant workers to normal family life; and
- assist in the development of African and black business enterprises, including distributors, suppliers of goods and services, and manufacturers.

As with the other points in the code, companies were graded by the consulting firm of Arthur D. Little on the basis of a written report required from each.

In 1983, a few of the US companies made some tentative efforts to lobby the government on noneconomic issues, a major breakthrough in practice. Specifically, the companies, through the American Chamber of Commerce in Johannesburg, protested a bill that would have, in effect, required employers to enforce influx-control laws in the workplace.

Pressures on the companies continued to mount. In 1983 the South African Council of Churches (SACC), a coalition of Protestant churches, passed a resolution asking the world community to refrain from investing in institutions that supported apartheid. In June 1983 Bishop Desmond Tutu, a former head of the SACC, proclaimed the Tutu "Principles." In November 1983 Sullivan announced the fourth amplification which largely followed the Tutu principles and required companies to lobby against apartheid laws. Notably, Sullivan's amplification differed from Tutu's principles in that he did not use the threat of withdrawal of all investment as leverage to move the government to dismantle apartheid. In November 1983, a large, black trade union coalition in the Republic of South Africa (COSATU), endorsed disinvestment. In 1985, meeting at a World Council of Churches (WCC) consultation in Harare, the SACC issued a definitive call for comprehensive economic sanctions until apartheid was dismantled. In November 1986 the fourth amplification was expanded and designated as principle seven of the Sullivan Principles. Principle seven is as follows:

- press for a single education system common to all races;
- use influence [to] support the unrestricted rights of black businesses to locate in the urban areas of the nation;
- influence other companies in South Africa to follow the standards of equal rights principles;
- support the freedom of mobility of black workers, including those from "so-called" independent homelands, to seek employment opportunities wherever they exist and make possible provision for adequate housing for families of employees within the proximity of workers' employment;
- use financial and legal resources to assist blacks, Coloreds, and Asians in their efforts to achieve equal access to all health facilities, educational institutions, transportation, housing, beaches, parks and all other accommodations normally reserved for whites;
- oppose adherence to all apartheid laws and regulations;
- support the ending of all apartheid laws, practices and customs; and
- support full and equal participation of blacks, Coloreds, and Asians in the political process.

Meanwhile, in 1984, Bishop Tutu was awarded the Nobel Peace Prize, and his campaign for economic sanctions against South Africa was given prominent global media coverage. All this additional pressure on the companies to leave South Africa no doubt influenced them in their willingness to support political rights for blacks. It is noteworthy that the 1984 Arthur D. Little report on the companies' progress on the principles includes the following observation on the new requirements of the program: "It is significant that there are today several areas in which companies are being requested to be active which would not have been tolerated by the companies when the program was initiated."[36]

In May 1985, in the face of enormous pressure at home and a rapidly deteriorating situation in South Africa, Sullivan announced an ultimatum: If statutory apartheid was not dismantled in two years, he would not continue to support the principles and would call for all companies to disinvest. While most US business leaders hoped that Sullivan would not issue such a call in 1987 (he did issue it in June 1987), the ultimatum pushed companies to be radical beyond their wildest dreams.

In June and August 1986 the US companies, in a watershed event, explicitly and publicly championed political rights in advertisements in major South African newspapers. Organized by the American Chamber of Commerce (AMCHAM), the advertisement proclaimed that "apartheid is totally contrary to the idea of free enterprise" and encouraged the government "to create a climate for negotiation." It listed the "urgent issues" that Pretoria must address: "Release political detainees; urban political organizations; negotiate with acknowledged leaders about power sharing; grant political rights to all; repeal the Population Registration Act; grant South African citizenship to all; repeal the Group Areas Act; provide common, equal education; and equalize health services."

The US companies that remained in South Africa took up the challenge and began to oppose the government on various fronts. Between 1986 and 1990 over 140 US companies departed South Africa under intense pressure at home. In 1990 the annual report on the activities of the US companies in South Africa, compiled by Arthur D. Little, Inc., as a part of the requirements of the Statement of Principles Program, notes that some 54 US companies continued to have operations there and that they provided more than $30 million a year to programs designed to eliminate apartheid. Some of these dollars were to assist in black educational endeavors, but many went to activities that most South Africans considered too risky because they directly challenged the status quo and advanced social change. For example, the Colgate

Palmolive Company provided the funds and personnel to organize a black consumer boycott of the stores in Boksburg after the local city council tried to restore segregation in the downtown city park. Other companies directly challenged white merchants in Johannesburg by assisting blacks in exercising their newly legislated freedom to do business in the downtown areas; this assistance was not only start-up funding, but also training in business skills and entrepreneurship.

Several companies such as the Kellogg Company used their influence and resources to secure the freedom of union leaders who were being detained by the police. Companies such as Johnson & Johnson also spent money to encourage nonracial education and medical care, a direct confrontation to the then-current structures based on a racial hierarchy. Many companies such as John Deere bought homes in white areas, making it possible for blacks to assume ownership, thus challenging and eroding the Group Areas Act that zoned land by race.[37]

What was happening here was clearly the breaking of the old mold and the fashioning of a new model. This new model holds much promise for the future of business, but only if it consciously appropriates the paradigm and takes a stand when human rights are violated. Because business never did this until late in the struggle in South Africa, activist groups never trusted the motives of the signatories of the Sullivan Principles and pressured the companies to leave right up to the 1990s. In 1995 there was some evidence that business had learned ethical language as, for example, in the cases of the "Levi Strauss & Co. Business Partner Terms of Engagement and Guidelines for Country Selection" policy and the "Caux Roundtable Principles for Business." Both of these codes explicitly advert to the importance of human rights in developing countries where business operations might be located. On the other hand, the ICCR members filed shareholder resolutions in 1995, asking three major multinational companies (Pepsi Co., Texaco, and Unocal) to include in their codes or policies how the corporation will deal with "decisions on investing in or withdrawing from countries where there is a pattern of ongoing and systematic violations of human rights."[38] Countries such as Burma, the People's Republic of China, Angola, Azerbaijan, Bahrain, Egypt, Indonesia, Nigeria, Saudi Arabia, and Turkey are all discussed in the Investor Responsibility Research Center (IRRC) report on the need for human rights guidelines for US companies.[39]

After considering a brief history of the struggle, it is now appropriate to consider some of the factors that made the changing paradigm and the development of the CSR issue especially compelling.

Integrating economic and social values in business: an idea whose time has come

To understand the American passion for political rights in South Africa, it is helpful to review some of the events that coalesced. Beginning in the mid-1960s, the civil rights movement took on a whole new dimension with the black power focus, and there emerged a new identification with the fate of the poor of the developing countries. From 1957 to 1964, 24 countries achieved independence in Africa. The ACOA formed a Committee of Conscience Against Apartheid and led a campaign against loans by US banks to South Africa. The ICCR, in the early 1970s, began a disinvestment campaign aimed at US corporations and banks. Campuses and church groups joined in the program.

In 1971 the Congressional black Caucus was formed with 13 black members of Congress. Congressman Diggs, chair of the House Subcommittee on Africa, had championed disinvestment as early as 1969.

Steve Biko, the popular anti-apartheid leader in South Africa, was murdered in September 1977, and this event mobilized widespread identification with the black cause. In July 1977 TransAfrica was chartered as an official lobby with a special focus on developing a more progressive US policy toward southern Africa. On 21 November 1984, Randall Robinson of TransAfrica began a protest at the South African Embassy and remained there until he was arrested. The protest lasted almost two years, with celebrities volunteering for a day and being arrested, events all graphically portrayed on the evening news. Over 2,000 people were arrested at the embassy during the two-year protest. As mentioned above, cities, states, and counties passed selective purchase ordinances, thus making foreign policy in the face of great dissatisfaction with the Reagan policy of constructive engagement. By 1986 most of the black leaders in South Africa argued for economic sanctions and disinvestment and saw little to be gained by constructive engagement.

Finally, on 2 October 1986, after exhausting a number of tactical moves, President Reagan found his veto overridden and the Comprehensive Anti-Apartheid Act of 1986 (Public Law 99-440) became law. The law strengthened the trade embargo and banned new loans and investments in South Africa until major signs that apartheid was dismantled were in evidence. Concerned with the issue of race in US foreign policy, Republican Senator Richard Lugar, chair of the Foreign Relations Committee, opposed Reagan and led the coalition with an override. The passage of this bill marked the culmination of a long struggle of the anti-apartheid organizations and the African-American coalitions.

It was many of these same coalitions that mounted the campaigns that ultimately forced the more than 100 US companies out of South Africa. A pervasive feeling remained in the movements that business was only interested in reaping profits in South Africa and that the principles were a cover story. The South African disinvestment saga taught most business leaders that they must listen to the public not only on economic issues but also on social issues. Integrating social and economic issues was becoming a new priority. In all fairness to business leaders, the period of the South African struggle with apartheid corresponded with a major rewriting of the implicit social contract between business and society.[40] Until relatively recently, market and legal signals were the only significant social forces that caught the attention of top management. Consumer sovereignty reigned to the extent that astute management carefully tracked consumer needs and expectations and responded with the appropriate product and price to capture the market in question. This market capitalism model had been a dominant one for more than two centuries.[41]

After the South Africa apartheid struggle there was a growing expectation that the social responsiveness of business must be much broader and is not optional. Advancing human rights was not based on a voluntary charity but rather on justice. Church coalitions and other activist groups critical of business in South Africa attributed their opposition to their interest in advancing a more humane and democratic society, a society that respected the rights of all. Yet it was not so long ago that there was a strong social consensus that the best way for business to advance a humane society was to compete efficiently in the market. Providing quality goods and services at the best price was taken to be business's contribution to the common good. During the South African controversy, from the 1950s to the 1980s, executives were living between the times—that is, they were caught between the time when there was a strong social consensus that the market and legal signals were the appropriate way to control business activity and the time when a new consensus was emerging that broadened the social contract with business. Some business leaders were quite astute and were aware of this significant sea change in the business environment. Many were challenged about their role in Vietnam, napalm production, or civil rights, for example. Yet perhaps because of a lack of adequate models and vocabulary, they were much less adept at forging the bonds of trust with the major critics of their South African operations.

Conclusion

To be sure, there is no claim here that the South African struggle was the catalyst that hastened the arrival of a new paradigm in business decision making. As indicated earlier in the chapter, scholars following important business leaders had been writing about the integration of economic and social values in business decision making on the part of some in business for almost 50 years before the South African apartheid struggle. In addition to the South Africa case, similar lessons could be gleaned from the apparel industry sweatshop struggle involving Nike and other major firms, or from the struggle that Shell had in Nigeria over the killing of Ken Saro-Wiwa and the repressive Abacha government with the Ogoni people in the Niger Delta. What seems clear is that today business, especially big business, is listening to the expectations of stakeholders and is often factoring those expectations into strategic planning and human rights policies. Nongovernmental organizations (NGOs) such as Amnesty International and Human Rights Watch now as a matter of course report on the human rights record of multinational firms in developing countries.[42] Most firms have learned the perils of being reactive to social pressure and are being proactive, scanning the environment for ethical issues and for issues that concern the public.

Archie B. Carroll, an important scholar in the field of CSR, notes that from the 1950s to the 1970s CSR literature was largely focused on defining the concept.[43] Carroll's conceptual framework understands a firm to be "socially responsible" only when it is fulfilling its obligations on three levels: economic (bottom line considerations); legal (complying with the legal system); and ethical (in accord with ethical principles). In this framework, the philanthropic activities are optional and in addition to the firm's ethical responsibilities. From the 1980s onward the field saw more research and the development of related themes. Stakeholder theory, business ethics theory, the concept of sustainability, and corporate citizenship are some of the major areas explored. In my view, similar to CSR, stakeholder theory, sustainability, and corporate citizenship are based on ethical values, primarily human rights, which guide managers on the obligations of a firm.

Stakeholder theory expands on the "social" in corporate social responsibility. To whom is the business responsible? Stakeholders! Popularized and developed by R. Edward Freeman,[44] the idea originated in the work of scholars who viewed business as interconnected with society rather than as an isolated entity.[45] Business has social responsibilities to its key stakeholders in addition to legal and financial ones. While scholars have differing views on the nature and extent of these responsibilities, and how to balance them, the concept of a stakeholder has enriched the discussion of CSR and its focus on human rights.

Corporate citizenship is often used as a synonym for CSR but its proper focus is on the rights and duties of a firm as part of society and is used in a fashion analogous to individual citizenship. Following the law, caring for the environment, making the community a better place, for example, are considered citizenship responsibilities.

The discipline of business ethics is based on moral philosophy and has seen hundreds of articles and textbooks in recent years. One of the important scholars in this area is Thomas Donaldson, who saw earlier than most that the responsibility for human rights is at the core of the discussion; this development is largely motivated by the belief that management is a normative discipline.[46] What is the right thing to do and how do I determine that? Did the multinational companies operating in South Africa have a moral obligation to champion human rights? Did apparel companies have a moral obligation to ensure that their subcontractors operating in developing countries did not run sweatshops? Business ethics argues that business should not only respect human rights in these situations but use its leverage to advance and protect human rights in the plants of its subcontractors. These and many other questions were new to business in the last 30 years and these issues spurred on the development of business ethics courses in many business schools throughout the globe. For many, the ethical assessment of business activity has enlarged the responsibility of business well beyond Friedman's "avoiding deception and fraud" and "following ethical custom."

In the new millennium, many argue the business case for CSR under the rubric "sustainability." Sustainability is the term most used by companies today to discuss their CSR activities. Similar to CSR, sustainability is difficult to define clearly. The term was first given prominence in the 1987 *Report on the World Commission on the Environment and Development*, the Brundtland Commission: "Sustainable development is development that meets the needs of the present without compromising the ability of the future generations to meet their own needs."[47] Here the primary focus was on the physical environment. So, for example, if a company was cutting down trees, it should plant a new tree for each one that was cut. Destroying the physical environment was unsustainable. Today the term has been broadened so that any activity that destroys the environment necessary for business success and long-term survival is considered unsustainable. The environment necessary for business long-term survival is thought to be not only the physical environment but also economic and governance issues as well as the social/ethical climate. Sustainability focuses on the long-term contribution of business to society and the impact of that activity on future generations. To give the reader an idea of how far we have come, consider the fact that at the beginning of the new millennium about a dozen of the Fortune 500 companies issued annual sustainability reports (or CSR, corporate citizenship or social responsibility reports). Today the great majority of these companies issue such reports. What is clear is that in the light of globalization and world trade, many business leaders, academics and stakeholders see that business should take a greater role in solving some of the social problems in the wider society. Business is not only responsible for its private good but also, to some extent, for the common good. In the final analysis, for business to flourish, society must flourish. To be sure, these new ideas were not greeted universally with enthusiasm by business scholars. Chapter 2 will discuss that controversy.

Notes

1 Andreas Georg Scherer and Guido Palazzo, "Toward a Political Conception of Corporate Social Responsibility: Business and Society Seen from a Habermasian Perspective," *Academy of Management Review* 32, no. 4 (2007): 1096–120.
2 Andrew Carnegie, *Autobiography of Andrew Carnegie* (Middlesex: The Echo Library, 1923).
3 John Mackey and Raj Sisodia, *Conscious Capitalism* (Cambridge, Mass.: Harvard Business Review Press, 2013).
4 Michael Kinsley, *Creative Capitalism: A Conversation with Bill Gates, Warren Buffett and Other Economic Leaders* (New York: Simon & Schuster, 2008).
5 Ben Cohen and Jerry Greenfield, with Meredith Moran, *Ben and Jerry's Double-Dip: Lead with Your Values and Make Money, Too* (New York: Simon & Schuster, 1997).
6 Howard R. Bowen, *Social Responsibilities of the Businessman* (New York: Harper & Row, 1953).
7 Morrell Heald, *The Social Responsibilities of Business: Company and Community 1900–1960* (New Brunswick, N.J.: Transaction Publishers, 1988).
8 Frank W. Abrams, "Management's Responsibilities in a Complex World," *Harvard Business Review* 29, no. 3 (1951): 29–34.
9 Benjamin M. Selekman, *A Moral Philosophy for Business* (New York: McGraw-Hill, 1959).
10 Richard Eells, *Corporate Giving in a Free Society* (New York: Harper & Brothers, 1956).
11 William C. Frederick, *Corporation Be Good: The Story of Corporate Social Responsibility* (Indianapolis, Ind.: Dog Ear Publishing, 2006).
12 Keith Davis, "Can Business Afford to Ignore Social Responsibilities?" *California Management Review* 2, no. 3 (1960): 70–76.

13 Joseph W. McGuire, *Business and Society* (New York: McGraw-Hill, 1963).

14 Clarence C. Walton, *Corporate Social Responsibilities* (Belmont, Calif.: Wadsworth, 1967).

15 Davis, "Can Business Afford to Ignore Social Responsibilities?" 71–73.

16 Committee for Economic Development, *Social Responsibilities of Business Corporations* (New York: CED, 1971).

17 Committee for Economic Development, *Redefining Government's Role in the Market System* (New York: CED, 1979).

18 George A. Steiner and John F. Steiner, *Business, Government, and Society*, 5th ed. (New York: Random House, 1988), 9.

19 Steiner and Steiner, *Business, Government, and Society*, 9.

20 The material presented here on the South Africa case study closely follows an earlier article of mine: Oliver F. Williams, "The Apartheid Struggle: Learnings from the Interaction between Church Groups and Business," in *Is the Good Corporation Dead: Social Responsibility in a Global Economy*, ed. John W. Houck and Oliver F. Williams (Lanham, Md.: Rowman & Littlefield, Inc., 1996), 203–29.

21 D. Kneale, "Xerox Finally Succumbs to Pressure," *Wall Street Journal*, 20 March 1987.

22 Interview with George Houser, 15 October 1994.

23 Steiner and Steiner, *Business, Government, and Society*, 9.

24 Jeffrey Pfeffer and J.R. Salancik, *The External Control of Organizations* (New York: Harper & Row, 1987), 106.

25 For a good discussion and illustration of the use of these strategic response patterns, see S. Prakash Sethi, *Multinational Corporations and the Impact of Public Advocacy on Corporate Strategy* (Boston, Mass.: Kluwer Academic Publishers, 1994), 34–39.

26 Timothy Smith, "Whitewash for Apartheid from Twelve U.S. Firms," *Business and Society Review* 74, no. 2 (1977): 59–60.

27 Letter from the Reverend Leon Sullivan to Mr George Houser, 25 April 1977. Unless otherwise indicated, all correspondence quoted here is from the Sullivan Principles Archives, Temple University, Philadelphia.

28 Letter from the Reverend Leon Sullivan to Father Robert C.S. Powell, 5 January 1977.

29 Letter from Sister Regina Murphy and 26 other members of the ICCR to General Motors, 31 October 1977.

30 "Pinching Apartheid," *New Republic*, 12 August 1985.

31 Letter from Henry Ford II to the Reverend Leon H. Sullivan, 11 November 1977, emphasis added.

32 Letter from R.H. Herzog to the Reverend Sullivan, 1 November 1976.

33 Sal G. Marzullo, Minutes of a Conference Board Meeting on South Africa, 15 March 1978.

34 Elizabeth Schmidt, *Decoding Corporate Camouflage: U.S. Business Support for Apartheid* (Washington, DC: Institute for Policy Studies, 1980).

35 Elizabeth Schmidt, "One Step—In the Wrong Direction: The Sullivan Principles as a Strategy for Opposing Apartheid," presentation to the State of Connecticut's Task Force on South African Investment Policy, 25 February 1982.

36 See Reid Weedon, *Eighth Report on the Signatory Companies to the Statement of Principles for South Africa* (Cambridge, Mass.: A.D. Little, 1984).

37 See the *Fourteenth Report on the Signatory Companies to the Statement of Principles for South Africa* (Cambridge, Mass.: A.D. Little, 1990).

38 See "U.S. Business and Human Rights Guidelines," *Social Issue Service: 1995 Background Report* (Washington, DC: Investor Responsibility Research Center, 1995), 1.

39 "U.S. Business and Human Rights Guidelines," 7–15.

40 For a discussion of the social contract between business and society, see Thomas Donaldson, *Corporations and Morality* (Englewood Cliffs, N.J.: Prentice-Hall, 1982), 50–53. See also Thomas Donaldson and Thomas W. Dunfee, *Ties That Bind: A Social Contracts Approach to Business Ethics* (Cambridge, Mass.: Harvard University Business School Press, 1999).

41 Steiner and Steiner, *Business, Government, and Society*, 9.

42 Human Rights Watch, *The Price of Oil: Corporate Responsibility and Human Rights Violations in Nigeria's Oil Producing Communities* (New York: Human Rights Watch, 1999), www.hrw.org/reports/1999/nigeria.

43 Archie B. Carroll, "Corporate Social Responsibility: Evolution of a Definitional Construct," *Business and Society* 38, no. 3 (1999): 268–95.

44 R. Edward Freeman, *Strategic Management: A Stakeholder Approach* (Boston: Pitman, 1984).

45 H. Igor Ansoff, *The New Corporate Strategy* (New York: Wiley and Sons, 1988); and Russell H. Ackhoff, *The Democratic Corporation* (Oxford: Oxford University Press, 1994).

46 Thomas Donaldson, *The Ethics of International Business* (Oxford: Oxford University Press, 1989). For this extensive literature, see the *Journal of Business Ethics* and *Business Ethics Quarterly*.

47 Brundtland Commission, *Report on the World Commission on the Environment and Development: Our Common Future*, www.un-documents.net/wced-ocf.htm.

2 The purpose of business
The basic issue

- **The South Africa case: an expanded role of business as a way to restore trust**
- **Milton Friedman: the market capitalism model**
- **What the scholars are saying**
- **The emerging purpose of business: creating value for all stakeholders**
- **The UN Principles for Responsible Management Education: an affirmation of the changing paradigm**
- **Conclusion**

From the 1950s until the new millennium, executives were living "between the times"—that is, they were caught between the time when there was a strong social consensus that the market mechanism was the best way to make the world a better place, and some possible future time when society would have a clear consensus about just how business institutions ought to advance human welfare. We are now searching for a new consensus: economic language, which has in the past often provided the sole rationale for corporate decisions, no longer, in itself, strikes a note of legitimacy for the public. While corporate critics speak in ethical language, employing terms such as fairness, justice, rights, and so on, corporate leadership often in the past responded solely in economic language of profit and loss. Such discussion generated much heat but little light, and the disputing parties passed like ships in the night.

Difficult questions are raised in deciding just what responsibility means in today's business climate. This chapter will attempt to give some answers to that question by considering some important scholars and business leaders. First the chapter summarizes how the South Africa case discussed in Chapter 1 caused leaders to focus on the purpose of business and whether and how to integrate economic and social values in their decisions as a way to restore trust. The next section will discuss

Milton Friedman's position, a position that has been the dominant view until the recent past. He argues that the sole purpose of business is to make profits. Although most surveys today find few business leaders who publicly espouse this position, there are scholars who are advocates and their work will be reviewed. Following this the chapter examines the range of opinions among scholars who favor an expanded purpose of business. Then the positions of two prominent business executives who have a new view of the role of business will be considered. A brief discussion of the United Nations Global Compact (UNGC) initiative for business schools, the Principles for Responsible Management Education (PRME), offers PRME's position on the purpose of business. The chapter concludes with this author's position.

The South Africa case: an expanded role of business as a way to restore trust

A brief review of the South Africa case study presented in Chapter 1 will help focus on the changing context and the gradual acceptance of a wider view of the purpose of the firm by many companies.[1] In 1987 Leon Sullivan, the well-known civil rights leader and pastor, asked me to serve on the board of directors of the Sullivan Principles for South Africa. As discussed in Chapter 1, these principles were formulated in a series of meetings involving numerous nongovernmental organizations (NGOs) (civil society members) and many companies that had operations in South Africa.[2] Finally, after much pressure on the companies, the principles were made more rigorous so that they actually did promote the human rights of blacks in South Africa. If a company wanted to remain in South Africa, the Sullivan Principles required that company to actively oppose all apartheid legislation and to promote and protect the civil and political rights of blacks in the workplace as well as the community. At its height, the Sullivan Principles had over 300 US companies as signatories. While the Sullivan Principles were not without controversy, for our purposes the significant point here is that the Sullivan Principles were the first instance of a shift from state-centric regulation to a new form of regulation created and implemented by the private sector and civil society. Opposing apartheid in South Africa was also the first instance where political ends were pursued by *directly* pressuring businesses without going through the government. NGOs, through their research and advocacy work, helped shape public opinion on the evils of apartheid. Up to this time, it was assumed that promoting and protecting civil, political, and social rights were the exclusive domains of the nation-state. What we observe here is the beginning of the demise of the strict division of labor between the private and public sectors. In large measure, this new role of business in society, advancing citizenship rights, was advocated by civil society because the government of South Africa was either unable or unwilling to do it on its own.

Leon Sullivan, the charismatic leader of the Sullivan Principles, advanced a compelling argument for companies assuming this new role in society. Sullivan was fond of telling the companies, "Where there is power, there is also responsibility."[3] Sullivan's point was not that companies had caused apartheid, or that they could buy legitimacy by dismantling it. Simply put, apartheid was wrong because it did not respect human dignity, it violated fundamental human rights. Because the companies had the economic power to dismantle it, they should do so. It should be clear that Sullivan was not arguing that the moral basis for the struggle against apartheid was founded on virtue, charity, or was in any way optional for the multinational companies operating in South Africa. Rather opposition to apartheid was based on justice; opposition was a moral imperative that was owed to those being deprived of fundamental human rights. It was the right thing to do. It is important to note that Sullivan was not offering a new version of "can implies ought," for the foundation of this moral obligation was not capability but the fact that human rights were being flagrantly violated. "Can," that is, the capability of business, was one of the criteria for assigning business the responsibility of working towards a remedy. The assumption of Sullivan was that there was a collective obligation of the moral community to dismantle apartheid and that multinational businesses in South Africa, because of their capability (and proximity), should be assigned a key role. If a company would not work to dismantle apartheid, Sullivan would publicly shame it and force it to leave South Africa. As discussed in Chapter 1, this notion that organizations that have power have to be accountable to society or else they lose their legitimacy is not new. In the business context, Keith Davis, in 1966, coined the phrase "the iron law of business responsibility."[4] In contemporary business literature the term *license to operate* is often used to convey the idea that society has certain expectations of business. If business does not meet those expectations, business loses its legitimacy, and there is a price to pay as a result. In the South African apartheid struggle, there are many examples of US society influencing the *license to operate* of companies perceived to be sustaining apartheid. For example, in the 1980s, 168 state, city, county, and regional authorities had some form of policy restricting their business dealings with US companies thought to be irresponsible in using their corporate power in South Africa.[5] Thus, the City of Chicago was precluded by one of these "selective purchasing ordinances" from buying buses from General Motors. GM understood the power of the people.

What we see in the South Africa case is that the "soft" transnational law complements "hard" national law, and the impetus for this law comes not from national political discussion but from transnational civil society. At least in practice, there is clearly a change underway in the way the responsibilities of the private and public sectors are apportioned. More reflection on one of the drivers of this recalibration may be helpful. One important factor in the expanded purpose of business, in business taking corporate social responsibility (CSR) much more seriously, is the recognition on the part of business of the crucial role of trust in a capitalist economy. When the cities and states passed the selective purchasing ordinances in the 1980s, thereby changing the terms of the license to operate, the root cause was a lack of trust in business and a growing divide between the values of business and those of society. This divide most often results in public pressure for additional regulation and legislation to control business, what economists call "transaction costs." Francis Fukuyama, in his important book on trust, shows how a low-trust society has higher transaction costs than a high-trust society, and he likens these costs to a kind of tax.[6] Perhaps the most dramatic example of a change in the social contract and of new transaction costs for business is the 2002 US Sarbanes-Oxley law enacted after the accounting scandals, which has increased auditing expenses 200 to 300 percent. The same might be said for the 2010 Dodd-Frank Wall Street Reform and Consumer Protection Act. The movement for CSR is, in large measure, a response to a decline in trust and an attempt to meet the legitimate expectations that society has for business.

Compared to 10 years ago, most surveys on trust levels in countries throughout the world show that public trust in business institutions and leadership is at a low level. Perhaps the most respected survey is that done under the leadership of the World Economic Forum (WEF),[7] an NGO funded by over 1,000 of the world's most influential corporations. The 2012 Edelman Trust Barometer surveyed citizens in 25 countries and found that only 47 percent trust business "to do what is right." In Ireland that number is 43 percent; the United Kingdom, 38 percent; South Korea, 31 percent; Germany, 34 percent; France, 28 percent; and the United States, 50 percent.[8]

What is the best way for corporations to restore and build new public trust in business? To answer this, it will be necessary to explore just what trust is and why it is given and withheld. The immediate causes of lack of trust in business are not difficult to catalogue: the financial crisis of the new millennium; financial frauds such as those at Enron, WorldCom, and Parmalat; corporate governance that approves exorbitant executive pay unrelated to performance; the volatility in world stock markets; and corporate deception, such as false dating of stock options. My concern, however, is to probe the underlying causes and nature of the trust deficit. A more comprehensive understanding of trust may also help us understand the move toward corporate citizenship and the changing role of business in society.

The work of Onora O'Neill, principal of Newnham College, Cambridge, is most helpful in probing the underlying nature of trust.[9] O'Neill suggests that placing and refusing trust is an age-old problem, and she refers us to the method of Socrates to clarify the issues. Active inquiry—asking questions and assessing answers, listening and checking information, or what is sometimes called the Socratic method—is the way we most often place or refuse trust. In O'Neill's view the calls for complete openness and global transparency, while possibly important values for a number of reasons, are not the best remedy for restoring trust. We need to follow the Socratic model and give people the opportunity to ask specific persons in business about specific information and specific actions that have been implemented. Through this process of active inquiry, a firm foundation for building and restoring trust is realized. Delving further into the nature of trust, the work of Mayer, Davis, and Schoorman in developing a model of trust in organizations helps us to understand why the method of Socratic active inquiry builds trust.[10] They define trust as the willingness of a party to be vulnerable to the actions of another party based on the expectations that the other will perform a particular action important to the trustor, irrespective of the ability to monitor or control that other party.[11] Thus, active inquiry serves to provide a rational basis for taking a risk, for making oneself vulnerable. The goal of their work is to highlight the reasons why one person would trust another—that is, what facilitates a trustor (trusting party) to trust a trustee (the party to be trusted)?

After an extensive review of the literature, Mayer, Davis, and Schoorman conclude that although numerous characteristics of the trustee enhance the development of trust in the trustor, these may all be related to three core characteristics: ability, benevolence, and integrity. Ability is defined as "that group of skills, competencies, and characteristics which enable a party to have influence within some specific domain." Benevolence is "the extent to which a trustee is believed to want to do good to the trustor." Integrity includes a strong sense of justice and fairness and is a part of character; it entails a trustee adhering "to a set of principles that the trustor finds acceptable."[12] Trustworthiness is conditioned on the perceptions that one has ability, benevolence, and integrity. If these core characteristics are perceived as high in a trustee, then a trustor will allow the personal vulnerability we commonly know as trust.

To be sure, trustworthiness is a continuum. When reports of polls speak of a decline in trust in corporations and their leaders, there is no implication here that people have lost all trust. Most are still purchasing products from these companies and many continue to invest in them.

What is being said, however, is that the perceptions of the characteristics and actions of business leaders by many people lead them to trust business less and to perceive that there is more risk involved in trusting behavior. This perception of greater risk leads many citizens to lobby for stronger organizational control systems, for example, the Dodd-Frank and the Sarbanes-Oxley laws. The irony here, however, is that such control systems may actually inhibit the development of trust since the good behavior of the business leader may now be perceived to be the result of the law rather than because of integrity or benevolence—that is, trustworthiness. People will begin to move to a more robust trust from a modest trust when trust (not control systems) actually yields good outcomes. When business leaders show by their actions that they actually have ability, benevolence, and integrity, then people will trust them more. Responsible corporate citizenship activities have the potential to enhance trust.

As a result of the South Africa case and other difficult interactions with stakeholders, many businesses realize that they are a crucial part of contemporary society and that trust is an essential dimension of capitalism. To recover trust many proactively reach out in a variety of CSR activities. These companies have a mission statement embodying societal expectations, including an acceptance of corporate citizenship, a widened purpose, and ethical values. I would underscore the expanded purpose of business espoused by these leading companies. Corporate citizenship activities, then, are a factor in building and maintaining trust because they enhance the perception that the firms have integrity and benevolence. Another method for building trust, however, is to have ongoing, open, and honest communication available for all interested stakeholders. Supporters and critics alike must know that they are able to engage in a dialogue with business officials and that they will be treated honestly and fairly. Such communication also ensures that this new political role of the firm is congruent with the democratic nature of society. For many in business, CSR activities are part of an expanded understanding of the purpose of business and an attempt to restore trust, to align the values of business with the values of society.

Milton Friedman: the market capitalism model

Some argue that morality and society's interests are served best by allowing the free market to produce and allocate resources; in this view, if the market encourages behavior that is undesirable to society, then the law is the appropriate tool to correct the situation. For those who take this position, market and legal signals are sufficient, and no moral or social constraints are appropriate. The basic responsibility of corporate leaders operating with this market mind-set is expressed well by one of its leading spokespersons, Milton Friedman: "to make as much money as possible while conforming to the basic rules of the society, both those embodied in law and those embodied in ethical custom."[13] For Friedman, "ethical custom" means the honesty, fidelity, and integrity required for the market mechanism to function. Ethical custom does not include bringing human and social values into economic decisions, but the integration of these concerns into the economic affairs of the corporation is precisely what is advocated by those concerned with the social responsibility of business. Quoting from his 1962 book *Capitalism and Freedom,*[14] Friedman states his position on the purpose of business in a widely quoted article titled "The Social Responsibility of Business is to Increase its Profits," published in the *New York Times Magazine.*[15]

> In a free-enterprise, private-property system, a corporate executive is an employee of the owners of the business. He has direct responsibility to his employers. That responsibility is to conduct the business in accordance with their desires, which generally will be to make as much money as possible while conforming to the basic rules of society, both those embodied in law and those embodied in ethical custom.
>
> ... there is one and only one responsibility of business—to use it (s) resources and engage in activities designed to increase its profits so long as it stays within the rules of the game, which is to say, engages in open and free competition without deception or fraud.[16]

Friedman does not discuss how the "basic rules of society" and even "ethical custom" are often significantly influenced by the lobbying efforts of business. Weak accounting standards and lax regulations of business lobbied for by business allowed the Enrons and WorldComs of our time to inflict much harm on society. Critics argue that business leaders must lobby for regulation that will enhance the community and not just increase profits.

Friedman argues that bringing human values into economic decisions will lead ultimately to a transfer of power from the market mechanism to the political mechanism, and that such excessive governmental power brings with it all the evils of socialism. Thus, he labels CSR as a "fundamentally subversive doctrine." His point on socialism is that if part of the purpose of business is to create value for stakeholders, gradually the power to control business will migrate to the government or to the people at large. Government may eventually want to regulate business to ensure that CSR is fairly administered. Yielding the social control of a company to the community is "fundamentally subversive" to the free enterprise system.

Instrumental CSR

In Friedman's philosophy of business, the purpose of business is to make money for the shareholders but this purpose may be advanced by pursuing so-called "social responsibility" endeavors. In his words:

> Of course, in practice the doctrine of social responsibility is frequently a cloak for actions that are justified on other grounds rather than a reason for those actions.
>
> To illustrate, it may well be in the long run interest of a corporation that is a major employer in a small community to devote resources to providing amenities to that community or to improving its government. That may make it easier to attract desirable employees, it may reduce the wage bill or lessen losses from pilferage and sabotage or have other worthwhile effects.
>
> In each of these and many similar cases, there is a strong temptation to rationalize these actions as an exercise of "social responsibility." In the present climate of opinion, with its wide spread aversion to "capitalism," "profits," the "soulless corporation" and so on, this is one way for a corporation to generate goodwill as a by-product of expenditures that are entirely justified in its own self-interest.[17]

For Friedman the only legitimate motivation for CSR on the part of a business is that it will enhance profits. This *instrumental* motivation of CSR stands in marked contrast to an *ethical* motivation where business works on some projects to advance the society at large because it believes it is the right thing to do and part of the purpose of business. This moral motivation for CSR may in fact yield greater profits because consumers may want to do business with a moral company but this enhanced profit is certainly not a sure thing.

When examining a company's CSR record it is often unclear what the motivation is. Reflecting on a company's mission statement, its core values and purpose, and whether it continues CSR projects even in an economic downturn may reveal what it actually stands for. What is clear is that the great majority of business leaders do not want to be identified with Friedman's philosophy of business. In a web-based survey of over 4,000 executives conducted by McKinsey & Co., respondents were asked if business should "focus solely on providing the highest possible return to investors while obeying all laws and regulations." Only 16 percent agreed with this philosophy.[18] The work of Googins, Mirvis, and Rochling on corporate citizenship supports similar findings.[19]

What the scholars are saying

For the most part, scholars and business leaders have found Friedman's position wanting, especially as the globalizing of the economy has brought multinational business to developing countries. Those arguing for a moral obligation for companies to improve the social environment beyond what is legally mandated or required by a duty to shareholders are certainly not in favor of putting a company's financial future in jeopardy.

My edited volume *Peace Through Commerce* has a chapter on "The Purpose of the Corporation" by Marilise Smurthwaite, which is a most comprehensive review of the literature and this will serve as my reference here.[20] Smurthwaite argues that all the literature on the purpose of business can be divided into five broad categories:

1 Make a profit for shareholders/owners;
2 Make a profit as well as develop individuals and serve the common good;
3 Make a profit and be a good citizen;
4 Make a profit while helping to form good human beings and contributing to community as a whole; and
5 Make a profit while being socially responsible, for example, projects relieving poverty.

Categories two to five all have an expanded understanding of the purpose of business and, for our concerns, they can be considered to embody the CSR perspective. Creating value has different shades of meaning.

Category one is, of course, well represented by Milton Friedman and is the classical liberal paradigm, what we have been calling the market capitalism model. Often known as "the financial theory of business," this position is espoused by such people as George Soros[21] and Elaine Sternberg.[22] Critics argue that some of the assumptions of the theory—an individualistic and mechanical conception of society, for example—are incorrect but the theory is still regarded as an important tool in finance.[23] As indicated earlier, most business leaders do not publicly espouse this position.

Category two authors speak of developing individuals and advancing the common good. The term common good refers to the sort of society where all individuals and groups have the opportunity to reach their fulfillment. This sort of society would be marked by respect for the dignity of the person, individual freedom, human interdependence and community and the right of each person to pursue his or her vocation. Poverty, health care, education, and so on, would be important issues. Catholic social thought in the 1991 document *Centesimus Annus* speaks of "the purpose of the business firm as not simply to make a profit, but it is to be found in its very existence as a *community of persons* who are endeavoring to satisfy their basic needs, and who form a particular group at the service of the whole society."[24] Stephen Porth,[25] Simon Zadek,[26] Robert G. Kennedy,[27] Helen Alford and Michael Naughton,[28] and Oliver Williams,[29] have this point of view.

Category three authors focus on good citizenship as part of the purpose of business. Kenneth Goodpaster argues that just as each individual has both a role responsibility (for example, as a husband, father, and lawyer), and also a citizenship responsibility (for example, paying taxes and volunteering to coach a children's team), so too does a business have both roles.[30] The "functional role" of business is to produce goods and services and the citizenship role is any of the various ways to advance the common good, discussed here as CSR. The later work of Archie Carroll has insightful contributions on being a good corporate citizen.[31] Sandra Waddock has made important contributions to this area as well.[32]

Category four focuses on those authors who discuss the role of business as one of developing virtuous people, people with those special qualities of character that enable a flourishing community. Called virtue ethics, the challenge for business is to form organizations that foster the development of good human beings. Robert C. Solomon[33] has been a prolific writer in this area.

Category five consists of the work of authors who explicitly use the term CSR or a related one in defining the purpose of business. Paul Samuelson and William D. Nordhaus,[34] James E. Post,[35] David A. Krueger,[36] Edward M. Epstein,[37] Thomas M. Jones,[38] Lee E. Preston,[39] S. Prakash Sethi,[40] Diane L. Swanson,[41] Donna J. Wood,[42] Steven L. Wartick,[43] Philip L. Cochran,[44] and other authors referenced in Chapter 1 are representative of this class.

The emerging purpose of business: creating value for all stakeholders

Chapter 1 spoke of the trajectory of CSR these last 70 years moving from a generalized corporate philanthropy aiding those external to the business, to a notion of creating sustainable value that involves all key stakeholders internal as well as external. Although this movement has been championed recently by academics, most notably Michael E. Porter and Mark R. Kramer,[45] it has long been practiced by astute business leaders. This section will largely focus on the business philosophy of John Mackey, CEO of Whole Foods,[46] with some discussion of Bill Gates, the founder and chairman of Microsoft and the Bill & Melinda Gates Foundation.[47]

As indicated in Chapter 1, Mackey is CEO of a company with a market capitalization of over US$8 billion. The company specializes in natural foods and has over 300 stores with sales of more than $4.5 billion and net profits of about $160 million each year. Mackey began the company over 35 years ago with $45,000 in capital. What is remarkable for our purposes, however, is not how well he has created shareholder value but the philosophy of business that guides his thinking. Similar to Peter Drucker, he sees pleasing the customer as "an end in itself" rather than a means to the end of maximizing profits.[48] However, the customer is only one stakeholder: "we measure our success by how much value we can create for all six of our most important stakeholders: customers, team members (employees), investors, vendors, communities, and the environment."[49] For Mackey, creating value for all of the stakeholders is the purpose of the firm. Friedman's position is not wrong, says Mackey, it is just too narrow and does not capture what business leaders actually do and why they do it.[50] While profit making is surely important, it is not the only purpose of business.

Mackey calls his philosophy *conscious capitalism* to call attention to the fact that he favors business leaders explicitly taking actions to advance the common good. For example, Whole Foods has historically donated 5 percent of the company's net profits to CSR projects in the community. Conscious capitalism is being contrasted with "hidden hand" capitalism, a view that the best way to develop society is to allow the free market to work without interference. This view supposedly represents Adam Smith's position. Adam Smith was the eighteenth-century moral philosopher who first helped the world understand how wealth was created in his famous *An Inquiry into the Nature and Causes of the Wealth of Nations*, sometimes called the "bible of capitalism."[51] In *The Wealth of Nations*, Smith sought to understand why some nations were wealthier than others. Part of his answer was that nations that encouraged free competitive markets were wealthier. In a curious kind of way, in the context of the economy, *when each person pursues his or her self-interest the common good is enhanced* and all are wealthier. Given competition, the baker bakes the very best bread possible and sells it at the lowest price feasible that will enable him to have the resources to buy what he wants. Competition unlocks creativity and innovation. Although motivated by self-interest, the result is that the community has good bread at a reasonable cost. Thus, Smith showed how economic self-interest is beneficial for the community.[52]

Making the case that the purpose of business is to create profits and that this is the best way for business to be socially responsible, Milton Friedman quotes Adam Smith: "By pursuing his own interest [an individual] frequently promotes that of society more effectually than when he really intends to promote it. I have never known much good by those who affected to trade for the public good."[53] However, without denying that self-interest can be an important motivation for unlocking creativity and innovation and thus creating better products and wealth for the community, Mackey draws on a more comprehensive reading of Adam Smith. He notes that in Smith's first book, *The Theory of Moral Sentiments*, it is clear that human nature is composed not only of self-interest but also of "sympathy, empathy, friendship, love, and the desire for social approval."[54] Thus the motivation for CSR can be consciously and deliberately to want to help the less fortunate even if there is no clear return to the business. Acknowledging the possibility of this moral motivation as opposed to merely an instrumental motivation for CSR is a key factor distinguishing Mackey from Friedman.

Friedman acknowledges that a business may want to "generate goodwill" by projects that are likely to be perceived as "socially responsible" but, make no mistake, this is "hypocritical window-dressing." The actual purpose of these projects is to increase profits says Friedman; this is what I have been calling instrumental social responsibility.

For Mackey, pursuing projects to help others can be motivated by the simple desire to do good, what I call moral social responsibility. Mackey's conscious capitalism can involve both instrumental and moral motivation but there certainly is no requirement that every action his business takes to help others must in some way yield more profits. Mackey's philosophy of business is clearly differentiated from Friedman's even though the two might be involved in identical actions.

For Mackey business is a high calling, a noble vocation, and its purpose is creating value for stakeholders. Value is not simply financial value although investors will require a good return. For employees value might be job security, education, and respect for work-life complexity; for customers it might be safe and quality products at a reasonable price; for the environment, it might be biodegradable packaging, low carbon processes, and pollution control; for communities it might mean taking measures to assist the least advantaged. Just as a medical doctor's purpose is to heal patients, a lawyer's purpose is to seek justice, and a teacher's is to educate, so too a manager's purpose is to create value for stakeholders. All these professions have to make money in order to continue but that is not their purpose.

While Mackey's philosophy of business may appear similar to Porter and Kramer's "shared value" concept, in my view there is a marked difference. Although Porter and Kramer describe admirably how business can address social concerns such as environmental pollution, public health, and the needs of the poor, they want to distance themselves from a moral stance. They argue for a capitalism in which "the ability to address societal issues is integral to profit maximization instead of treated as outside the profit model."[55] If the motivation in their model is only instrumental and never moral, then this philosophy of business differs from Mackey's.

There is no question that much good can come from Porter and Kramer's creating shared value strategy. Steve Lohr in *The New York Times* discusses how General Electric's "ecomagination" program designed to produce products that required less energy as well as less water increased profits for GE by almost 80 percent. Customers were concerned about carbon emissions and fuel costs and GE responded with more sustainable products. GE's CEO Jeffrey R. Immelt offered this assessment: "We did it from a business standpoint from day 1. It was never about corporate responsibility."[56] This stance is surely an advance over past corporate strategy and, although I would call it instrumental CSR, it is an important contribution to creating sustainable value.

I have selected Mackey to discuss the changing paradigm of the purpose of business because he is not only an astute business leader but also a gifted speaker and writer. Unlike many executives, he has the ability to articulate his philosophy of business in a compelling fashion. It should be clear, however, that he is only one of a growing number of contemporary business leaders who embrace creating value for stakeholders as the purpose of business. Howard Schultz of Starbucks, Herb Kelleher of Southwest Airlines, Bill George of Medtronic, Ratan N. Tata of Tata Sons, Biz Stone of Twitter are only a few of this growing number. What is remarkable about these contemporary executives is not that they wanted a new understanding of the purpose of business but rather that they actually brought this new stakeholder perspective into corporate strategic planning and created value across the board.

Chapter 1 discussed the visionary Frank Abrams who over 60 years ago articulated a very similar philosophy of business but as CEO of a major oil company he had only modest success in actually changing his company. With the globalization of the economy and the huge expansion of the business sector in the last 60 years, society expects business to consider major stakeholders and to integrate environmental, social and governance (ESG) issues into its strategic planning. Had Abrams been running the company today, it would very likely look like Whole Foods or Starbucks.

Another important leader in the movement toward a broader understanding of the role of business in society is Bill Gates. In a 2008 address to the WEF in Davos, Switzerland, Gates outlined his philosophy of business called "creative capitalism."[57] Obviously Gates is very supportive of capitalism noting all the prosperity it has delivered to people around the globe but he is concerned about the billion very poor people who are essentially left out of the economic developments. We need "system innovation" in the capitalist world to bring about market-driven efforts that would hasten the elimination of poverty, says Gates. Quoting Adam Smith, he reminds us that self-interest is only one of two motivations deeply rooted in our human nature. The other is "caring for others." Over 235 years ago, Smith commented: "How selfish soever man may be supposed, there are evidently some principles in his nature, which interest him in the fortunes of others, and render their happiness necessary to him, though he derives nothing from it, except the pleasure of seeing it." From his experience, Gates argues that "positive recognition" is a market-based incentive and that caring for others is its own reward.

For Gates, efforts to assist the least advantaged are not a new idea since over the past 20 years Microsoft has donated more than $3 billion in cash and software, and has developed management skills in less developed areas. The company also provides time for its researchers to work on new products for those with little education and literacy. These efforts may enhance the company's reputation, attract customers and appeal to highly qualified potential employees. If so, all well and good. Gates cites a number of projects where business is practicing "creative capitalism," such as "tiered pricing" in the pharmaceutical industry and the Bono ("RED" campaign) initiative to raise money for the poor. He appeals to all companies to get involved. "If we can spend the early decades of the twenty-first century finding approaches that meet the needs of the poor in ways that generate profits and recognition for business, we will have found a sustainable way to reduce poverty in the world."

The UN Principles for Responsible Management Education: an affirmation of the changing paradigm

The UN Global Compact (UNGC) was launched by the then secretary-general of the United Nations, Kofi Annan, in 2000 and businesses throughout the world were invited to join.[58] To join, a business had to agree to bring the 10 principles concerning human rights, labor issues, environmental concerns, and anti-corruption issues into its strategic planning. As of March 2013 over 7,000 businesses in 135 countries have become signatories. More reflection on the UNGC will follow in Chapter 4 but for now an organization sponsored by the compact, the Principles for Responsible Management Education (PRME), is our focus.[59]

What became clear after the first few years of operating the UNGC was that many executives were ill-equipped to be leaders in the movement to advance human rights, the environment and anti-corruption programs. Based on recommendations of academic and business leaders, an international task force was formed consisting of 60 members—deans, university presidents, and official representatives of leading business schools. The task force was charged to provide a framework for academic institutions to advance corporate social responsibility through the incorporation of universal values into curricula and research. The result was the formation of PRME, which was launched at the 2007 Global Compact Leaders Summit on 5 July in Geneva, Switzerland. Today PRME has almost 500 of the world's best business schools as members. The text and principles of PRME are as follows:

> As institutions of higher education involved in the development of current and future managers we declare our willingness to progress in the implementation, within our institution, of the following

Principles, starting with those that are more relevant to our capacities and mission. We will report on progress to all our stakeholders and exchange effective practices related to these principles with other academic institutions:

Principle 1
Purpose: We will develop the capabilities of students to be future generators of sustainable value for business and society at large and to work for an inclusive and sustainable global economy.

Principle 2
Values: We will incorporate into our academic activities and curricula the values of global social responsibility as portrayed in international initiatives such as the United Nations Global Compact.

Principle 3
Method: We will create educational frameworks, materials, processes and environments that enable effective learning experiences for responsible leadership.

Principle 4
Research: We will engage in conceptual and empirical research that advances our understanding about the role, dynamics, and impact of corporations in the creation of sustainable social, environmental and economic value.

Principle 5
Partnership: We will interact with managers of business corporations to extend our knowledge of their challenges in meeting social and environmental responsibilities and to explore jointly effective approaches to meeting these challenges.

Principle 6
Dialogue: We will facilitate and support dialogue and debate among educators, students, business, government, consumers, media, civil society organizations and other interested groups and stakeholders on critical issues related to global social responsibility and sustainability.

We understand that our own organizational practices should serve as an example of the values and attitudes we convey to our students.

The significant issue for our study is that when it came to defining just what the purpose of business is, what we are educating young men and women to do, there was clear consensus as reflected in Principle 1: " ... to be future generators of sustainable value for business and society at large ..." Echoing Mackey's "conscious capitalism" and Gates's "creative capitalism," the document goes on to advocate working "for an inclusive and sustainable global economy." The goal is to have 1,000 signatory business schools in PRME by 2015 and by all accounts this will be realized. It seems clear that the paradigm shift from the market capitalism model to the business ecology model is an accomplished fact in the academy. Whether this is the case for business will be discussed in later chapters.

Conclusion

A crucial insight of Howard Bowen in his 1953 book *Social Responsibilities of the Businessman* is that the values of business must, in large measure, mirror the values of society.[60] When there is a gap between what business is doing and the expectations of society, there is a loss of trust and increasing regulation. Frank Abrams in his 1951 article captured the insight that has motivated a great many of the scholars and practitioners who have followed him: "Public approval is no less essential to the continued existence of today's kind of business than adequate capital, or efficient management."[61] All the evidence indicates that the advice of Bowen and Abrams has not been heeded. A 1999 poll by Environics International (now called GlobeScan International), titled The Millennium Poll on Corporate Social Responsibility, questioned 25,000 people in 23 countries about CSR. Two-thirds of the respondents wanted companies to go beyond their traditional roles ("make profit, pay taxes, create jobs & obey all laws") and assume a broader role ("set higher ethical standards and help build a better society").[62] The 2012 Edelman Trust Barometer, on the basis of over 30,000 respondents in 25 countries, reported that business is not meeting the expectations of the public.[63] There is a significant gap between what business is doing and what the public expects. According to the Edelman study, business is failing to meet public expectations in the following areas: placing customers ahead of profits, treating employees well, listening to customers' needs and feedback, having ethical business practices, having transparent and open business practices, working to protect and improve the environment, addressing society's needs in everyday business, and creating programs that positively impact the local community in which the company operates. The report suggests that it is in the self-interest of business to be a proactive leader in CSR.

Keith Davis's iron law of responsibility (Where there is power there is also responsibility), discussed in Chapter 1, is a helpful way to understand the moral argument for CSR, the rising expectations of society and the paradigm shift from the market capitalism model to the business ecology model.[64] Astute business leaders have risen to the challenge and embraced a broader purpose of business in society. John Mackey and Bill Gates exemplify what success looks like in this new role. Academic associations such as PRME have ratified and developed the purpose of business as the creation of sustainable value, and in my view they are correct. Even with all of this, there is much that remains to be done. The chapters that follow will continue to chart a way to realize the vision of a better life for all.

Notes

1 This discussion of South Africa closely follows an earlier article of mine: Oliver F. Williams, "Responsible Corporate Citizenship and the Ideals of the United Nations Global Compact," in *Peace Through Commerce*, ed. Oliver F. Williams (Notre Dame, Ind.: University of Notre Dame Press, 2008), 432–34, 439–42.

2 S. Prakash Sethi and Oliver F. Williams, *Economic Imperative and Ethical Value in Global Business: The South African Experience and International Codes Today* (Notre Dame, Ind.: University of Notre Dame Press, 2001). See also Oliver F. Williams, *The Apartheid Crisis: How We Can Do Justice in a Land of Violence* (San Francisco, Calif.: Harper & Row, 1986).

3 Sethi and Williams, *Economic Imperative and Ethical Value in Global Business*, xii.

4 Keith Davis and Robert Blomstrom, *Business and its Environment* (New York: McGraw-Hill, 1966).

5 Sethi and Williams, *Economic Imperative and Ethical Value in Global Business*, 295–97.

6 Francis Fukuyama, *Trust: The Social Virtues and the Creation of Prosperity* (New York: Free Press, 1995).

7 Geoffrey Allen Pigman, *The World Economic Forum* (London: Routledge, 2007).

8 *The 2012 Edelman Trust Barometer*, www.trust.edelman.com.

9 Onora O'Neill, *A Question of Trust: The BBC Reith Lectures* (Cambridge: Cambridge University Press, 2002).

10 R.C. Mayer, J.H. Davis, and F.D. Schoorman, "An Interactive Model of Organizational Trust," *Academy of Management Review* 20, no. 3 (1995): 709–34.

11 Mayer *et al.*, "An Interactive Model of Organizational Trust," 712.

12 Mayer *et al.*, "An Interactive Model of Organizational Trust," 714.

13 Milton Friedman, "The Social Responsibility of Business is to Increase its Profits," *The New York Times Magazine*, 13 September 1970, www.colorado.edu/studentgroups/libertarians/issues/friedman-soc-resp-business.html.

14 Milton Friedman, *Capitalism and Freedom* (Chicago, Ill.: University of Chicago Press, 1962).
15 Friedman, "The Social Responsibility of Business is to Increase its Profits."
16 Friedman, "The Social Responsibility of Business is to Increase its Profits," 4. This quote is from Milton Friedman, *Capitalism and Freedom*, 60–61.
17 Friedman, "The Social Responsibility of Business is to Increase its Profits," 3.
18 "Global Survey of Business Executives: Business and Society," *The McKinsey Quarterly*, January 2006, www.mckinseyquarterly.com.
19 Bradley K. Googins, Philip H. Mirvis, and Steven A. Rochlin, *Beyond Good Company: Next Generation Corporate Citizenship* (New York: Palgrave Macmillan, 2007), 27–29.
20 Marilise Smurthwaite, "The Purpose of the Corporation," in *Peace Through Commerce*, ed. Oliver F. Williams (Notre Dame, Ind.: University of Notre Dame Press, 2008), 13–54. Another important contribution to the literature is Archie B. Carroll, "Corporate Social Responsibility: Evolution of a Definitional Construct," *Business & Society* 38, no. 3 (1999): 268–95.
21 George Soros, *Open Society: Reforming Global Capitalism* (London: Little, Brown and Company, 2000), 161.
22 Elaine Sternberg, *Just Business: Business Ethics in Action* (Oxford: Oxford University Press, 2000), 32.
23 Charles M.A. Clark, "Competing Visions: Equity and Efficiency in the Firm," in *Rethinking the Purpose of Business*, ed. S.A. Cortright and Michael J. Naughton (Notre Dame, Ind.: University of Notre Dame Press, 2002), 87.
24 Pope John Paul II, *Centesimus Annus* (Washington, DC: U.S. Catholic Conference, 1991), para. 35.
25 For a good discussion of the principles of Catholic social thought, see Stephen J. Porth, David Steingard, and John McCall, "Spirituality and Business: The Latest Management Fad or the Next Breakthrough?" in *Business, Religion, and Spirituality*, ed. Oliver F. Williams (Notre Dame, Ind.: University of Notre Dame Press, 2003), 255–60.
26 Simon Zadek, *The Civil Corporation: The New Economy of Corporate Citizenship* (London: Earthscan, 2004), 138–40.
27 Robert G. Kennedy, "The Virtue of Solidarity and the Purpose of the Firm," in *Rethinking the Purpose of Business*, ed. S.A. Cortright and Michael J. Naughton (Notre Dame, Ind.: University of Notre Dame Press, 2002), 57–67.
28 Helen J. Alford and Michael J. Naughton, "Beyond the Shareholder Model of the Firm: Working Toward the Common Good of a Business," in *Rethinking the Purpose of Business*, ed. Cortright and Naughton, 29–35.
29 Oliver F. Williams, "Is it Possible to Have a Business Based on Solidarity and Mutual Trust? The Challenge of Catholic Social Teaching to Capitalism and the Promise of Southwest Airlines," *Journal of Catholic Social Thought* 9, no. 1 (2012): 59–69. For additional articles and books, see www.nd.edu/~ethics.
30 Kenneth E. Goodpaster, "Can a Corporation be a Citizen?" *Praxis* 2, no. 3 (2001): 2–7.
31 Archie B. Carroll, "The Pyramid of Corporate Social Responsibility: Toward the Moral Management of Organizational Stakeholders," *Business Horizons* 34, no. 4 (1991): 39–48.

32 Sandra Waddock, *Leading Corporate Citizens: Vision, Values, Value-Added*, 3rd ed. (New York: McGraw-Hill, 2009).

33 Robert C. Solomon, "Business with Virtues: Maybe Next Year?" *Business Ethics Quarterly* 10, no. 1 (2000): 340–60.

34 Paul Samuelson and William D. Nordhaus, *Economics*, 12th ed. (New York: McGraw-Hill, 1985).

35 James E. Post, Lee E. Preston, and Sybille Sachs, *Redefining the Corporation* (Stanford, Cal.: Stanford University Press, 2002).

36 David A. Krueger, *The Business Corporation and Productive Justice* (Nashville, Tenn.: Abingdon Press, 1997).

37 Edward M. Epstein, "The Corporate Social Policy Process: Beyond Business Ethics, Corporate Social Responsibility, and Corporate Social Responsiveness," *California Management Review* 29, no. 3 (1987): 99–114.

38 Thomas M. Jones, "Corporate Social Responsibility Revisited, Redefined," *California Management Review* 22, no. 3 (1980): 59–67.

39 Post, Preston, and Sachs, *Redefining the Corporation*.

40 S. Prakash Sethi, "Moving from a Socially Accountable Corporation," in *Is the Good Corporation Dead? Social Responsibility in a Global Economy*, ed. John W. Houck and Oliver F. Williams (Lanham, Md.: Rowman & Littlefield Publishers, 1996), 83–100.

41 Diane L. Swanson, "Addressing a Theoretical Problem by Reorienting the Corporate Social Performance Model," *Academy of Management Review* 20, no. 1 (1995): 43–64.

42 Donna J. Wood, "Corporate Social Performance Revisited," *Academy of Management Review* 16, no. 4 (1991): 691–718.

43 Steve L. Wartick and Philip L. Cochran, "The Evolution of the Corporate Social Performance Model," *Academy of Management Review* 10, no. 4 (1985): 758–69.

44 Wartick and Cochran, "The Evolution of the Corporate Social Performance Model."

45 Michael E. Porter and Mark R. Kramer, "Strategy & Society: The Link Between Competitive Advantage and Corporate Social Responsibility," *Harvard Business Review* 84, no. 12 (2006): 78–92.

46 John Mackey and Raj Sisodia, *Conscious Capitalism: Liberating the Heroic Spirit of Business* (Cambridge, Mass.: Harvard Business Review Press, 2013).

47 Bill Gates, "A New Approach to Capitalism," in *Creative Capitalism: A Conversation with Bill Gates, Warren Buffett and Other Economic Leaders*, ed. Michael Kinsley (New York: Simon & Schuster, 2008), 7–39.

48 Peter F. Drucker, "The New Meaning of Corporate Social Responsibility," *California Management Review* 26, no. 2 (1984): 53–63.

49 John Mackey, Milton Friedman, and T.J. Rodgers, "Rethinking the Social Responsibility of Business," reason.com/archives/2005/10/01/rethinking-the-social-responsi.

50 Mackey *et al.*, "Rethinking the Social Responsibility of Business."

51 Adam Smith, *The Wealth of Nations*, 5th ed., ed. Edwin Cannan (London: Methuen, 1904 [1776]).

52 See Patricia H. Werhane, "Business Ethics and the Origins of Contemporary Capitalism: Economics and Ethics in the Work of Adam Smith and Herbert Spencer," *Journal of Business Ethics* 24, no. 3 (2000): 185–98; and

Oliver F. Williams, "Catholic Social Teaching: A Communitarian Democratic Capitalism for the New World Order," *Journal of Business Ethics* 12, no. 12 (1993): 919–23.

53 Mackey *et al.*, "Rethinking the Social Responsibility of Business," 4.

54 Mackey *et al.*, "Rethinking the Social Responsibility of Business," 3. See Adam Smith, *The Theory of Moral Sentiments*, 6th ed. (London: A. Millar, 1790).

55 Quoting Michael Porter in Steve Lohr, "First, Make Money. Also, Do Good," *The New York Times*, 13 August 2011. See also Michael E. Porter and Mark R. Kramer, "Creating Shared Value: How to Reinvent Capitalism—and Unleash a Wave of Innovation and Growth," *Harvard Business Review* 89, nos. 1–2 (2011): 1–17.

56 Lohr, "First, Make Money. Also, Do Good."

57 Gates, "A New Approach to Capitalism," 7–16.

58 See the website: www.unglobalcompact.org.

59 See the website, www.unprme.org. On the website is *The PRME Inspirational Guide* which features 63 case stories from 47 institutions representing 25 countries and provides a good overview of what business schools are doing.

60 Howard R. Bowen, *Social Responsibilities of the Businessman* (New York: Harper & Row, 1953).

61 Frank W. Abrams, "Management's Responsibilities in a Complex World," *Harvard Business Review* 29, no. 3 (1951): 29–34, at 30.

62 The poll discussed here is available at: www.globescan.com/news_archives/MPExecBrief.pdf.

63 2012 Edelman Trust Barometer, trust.edelman.com.

64 Keith Davis, "Five Propositions for Social Responsibility," *Business Horizons* 18, no. 3 (1975): 19–24. Republished in Archie B. Carroll, ed., *Managing Corporate Social Responsibility* (Boston, Mass.: Little, Brown and Company, 1977), 46–51.

3   Stretching the limits of CSR

Breaking the bounds of the market logic

- **The market for virtue approach and its critics**
- **John Ruggie's approach to business and human rights: missing a teachable moment**
- **The creation of value approach**
- **Conclusion**

This chapter explores how we might encourage more companies to participate and bring corporate social responsibility (CSR) up to scale so that business could make a substantial contribution to a sustainable future for all. There are at least two ongoing debates about the role of CSR in business. The first concerns the motivation for CSR activities on the part of business. Is it always true that a business case can be made for CSR? Is it always possible to do well while doing good? Two prominent scholars, David Vogel and Bill Frederick, each have opposing views on this point and their perspectives will be discussed. Vogel argues that most companies will be involved in CSR only when it makes business sense and hence without more pressure from civil society and legally binding rules from government, CSR has a limited future. Frederick argues that other values besides the market can be and are a driver for CSR and he is confident that the march toward CSR will continue.

The second issue for this chapter concerns determining the best way to motivate business to practice CSR—in particular, to practice respect for human rights. Is it by making a business case for respecting human rights or a moral case? To bring this issue into focus the recent work of John Ruggie will be considered. To be sure, Ruggie's charge was not to suggest the best way to motivate people to honor human rights but an unintended side effect of his work was to slight the moral case for CSR. Ruggie was the special representative of the UN secretary-general for business and human rights and was tasked with defining exactly what the obligations are for business in regards to human rights. He was commissioned to do this work because the business community had misgivings about a United Nations (UN) subcommittee proposal at the start of the millennium that equated business's responsibility with that of the state. After five years of research, Ruggie proposed the formula: protect, respect, and remedy. Business was to make sure that it was in no way adversely affecting the human rights of stakeholders. His main justification was that interfering in the human rights of others was "doing harm," and that this harm would eventually damage the reputation of business and have adverse economic impacts on business. In the words of Chapter 2, avoiding the violation of human rights was functional CSR (it may hurt the bottom line), without any reference to moral CSR (it is the wrong thing to do). To be fair, it should be clear that Ruggie's central point is that the obligations for business are limited. Governments have the duty to protect and promote human rights while business has to respect them—that is, make sure it does not in any way violate the rights of others. Both have the duty to set up processes to adjudicate allegations of rights violations. For the purposes of our study, the key point is that Ruggie is not making a moral argument that business ought to avoid violating human rights but rather one based on the logic of the business system. Thus for Ruggie the best driver for CSR (respecting human rights) is the pressure from non-governmental organizations (NGOs), loss of reputation, and consequent harm to the financial bottom line.

Chapter 2 discussed the purpose of business as the creation of value for all stakeholders and this chapter expands on that reflection and suggests that it is also the best way to stretch the limits of CSR. Finally, the chapter concludes arguing that a version of business as a sustainable value creator holds much promise to fashion a better world for all.

The market for virtue approach and its critics

David Vogel authored a most insightful book titled *The Market for Virtue: The Potential and Limits of Corporate Social Responsibility*.[1] In the conclusion, Vogel cites Jeffrey Hollender of Seventh Generation as a way to summarize his main thesis:

> While there are still valid market forces inducing companies to be better corporate citizens, those market forces alone are rarely adequate to effect necessary change. Market forces, when they work, often produce cheaper and more innovative solutions to social and environmental problems, but that in and of itself will not provide an acceptable solution to the problems we face.[2]

Vogel argues that if we want to fashion a better society, advancing social and environmental values, then some of the voluntary standards of CSR must be made legally binding. He is not denying that civil regulation, "soft law," has made significant advances but rather is outlining what the next step should be. He states this well:

> It would be better if China enforced its labor laws, but even if the government fails to act, Mattel can improve conditions for some Chinese workers. It would be better if Vietnam had more stringent occupational safety and health standards, but in their absence, thanks to Nike, some workers are exposed to fewer hazards. It would be better if the Indian government provided schools for all the country's children, but at least Ikea and Rugmark Foundation can give more Indian children access to education. It would be better if the United States imposed legally binding restrictions on emissions of greenhouse gases, but since it has been unwilling to do so, voluntary corporate programs are better than nothing.[3]

For Vogel, one of the major tasks of corporate responsibility is to influence public policy so that all firms are required to be more responsible. Government rule making along with increased NGO and stakeholder social pressure are the tools necessary to bring CSR up to scale. Virtue does not "pay off" so CSR will never be attractive to many businesses.

The Vogel study has excellent chapters on three key areas of CSR: working conditions in developing countries, the environment, and human rights and global corporate citizenship. Examining the many studies concerning whether CSR yields higher profits, he concludes that CSR is "largely irrelevant to financial performance."[4] A small number of firms have created a niche market and built CSR into their corporate strategy. Vogel mentions, among others, Patagonia and Starbucks. He cautions, however, that business should not expect to be rewarded by the market for responsible behavior. Those who argue that CSR is crucial for success in business today are not supported by the evidence.

Robert Reich is much more strident than Vogel, calling CSR a dangerous distraction.[5] It is the government's role to solve social problems and the lobbying efforts of business are often directed against the very laws that would serve the public interest. While Reich certainly makes some good points in *Supercapitalism*, it is difficult to understand why any role of business in solving social problems is discouraged. Especially in developing countries, governments are often unable or unwilling to tackle these social issues. The global economy does not have any effective global governance so often the best alternative is a set of soft laws, emerging international standards, for example, the 10 principles of the United Nations Global Compact (UNGC), which guide multinational companies.

Some would question whether a key assumption of both Vogel and Reich is correct. Is it true that the logic of the market is the controlling logic of all business leaders who espouse CSR? Are they only doing CSR projects to maximize profits? Or are they trying to manage a business with an expanded purpose, a dual logic, the market capitalism logic and a CSR logic, trying to make money for investors while at the same time trying to create "wealth" for other stakeholders, with the latter goal not being subservient to the former? In the earlier chapters I called this dual logic the business ecology model. What is clear for Vogel is that the way to increase the number of companies involved with CSR is to demonstrate the business case more effectively, to have more government regulation and to increase the pressure from NGOs and civil society.

William (Bill) Frederick, another major scholar in the field, assuming an expanded purpose of business, disagrees with Vogel: "A firm's commercial gain from social activity is literally beside the point and is no measure of its social responsibility. The market and business profit-seeking, register only part of a more complex process of values transformation."[6] CSR may or may not enhance a firm's economically productive role. CSR activities that enhance life both for the firm and for the people in the wider society have value, although perhaps not financial value for investors. If the purpose of business is to create value for stakeholders, then CSR activities that do so are part of the purpose.

The division of thought here is between those holding the traditional view of business where responsible conduct, CSR activities, are done to ensure profit, and those holding the new paradigm. The new paradigm does not see CSR as a tool to enhance profit generation (although it may), but rather sees business as having a threefold challenge: economic, social and environmental. All three dimensions are valid parts of the purpose of business and guide business decisions and projects. The notion that business does not have a sole financial purpose but rather a broader purpose is captured with the term *triple bottom line*, economic, social and environmental (TBL). This idea has been evolving over the history of CSR and has only gained prominence in recent years. John Elkington in his 1997 book *Cannibals with Forks: The Triple-Bottom Line of 21st Century Business* has given us the vocabulary and framework for thinking about CSR in the new paradigm but some business leaders have been practicing it for years. John Mackey and Bill Gates are two leaders of this development discussed in Chapter 2. Elkington has popularized the term "triple bottom line," and encouraged more and more firms to develop social and environmental accounting for the benefit of investors, activists and other stakeholders.[7] The Global Reporting Initiative (GRI) is an NGO organized to develop a common metric for reporting social and environmental issues.[8] Today this set of questions is widely used by business.

As indicated in Chapter 1, the initial call was for business to factor social issues into business decisions. Leon Sullivan and Frank Abrams, for example, did not see environmental issues as crucial for business. The 1987 Brundtland Report was a wake-up call for business to pay attention to the natural environment, and subsequent UN meetings in Rio de Janeiro (the Earth Summit) in 1992, in Johannesburg (World Summit on Sustainable Development) in 2002, and in Rio de Janeiro (Rio + 20 Corporate Sustainability Forum) in 2012, put environmental issues squarely on the business agenda. To give an idea of how rapidly the concern for TBL developed, in 1995 only a handful of businesses had triple bottom line reports. Today almost all major companies have such reports (sometimes called sustainability reports, corporate citizenship reports, corporate social responsibility reports, people, planet, and profit reports, and so on).

The point of this discussion for our study is to highlight the fact that social and environmental considerations were not thought to be subservient to financial considerations but that all three concerns were on equal footing. Leon Sullivan and other anti-apartheid activists never argued that business should oppose apartheid so that it could make more money, but rather because it was the right thing to do. Even if a company's opposition to apartheid would result in some loss of profit, it still should be done. At least in some cases, CSR is not being embraced simply because it will enhance return on investment based on a business case that projects in the area of social and environmental concerns will contribute to a firm's financial position. CSR may be motivated by a concern to create value for all stakeholders, especially the least advantaged. Frederick believes that we will see many more businesses in the movement, not because it will yield greater profits (although it may), but rather because it is the right thing to do, it is part of the very purpose of business. Several quotes from business leaders may illustrate this point. A CEO of GlaxoSmithKline (GSK) put it this way:

Some months ago, when the newly emerged GlaxoSmithKline was formed, I said that I did not want to be head of a company that caters only to the rich. I made access to medicines in poorer countries a priority and I take this opportunity to renew that pledge. We have 11,000 people who go to work every morning because they are pro-public health. We have to make a profit for our shareholders but the primary objective of any policy put forward in the industry is public health.[9]

In a similar way, Starbucks combines the normative case with the business case:

Consumers are demanding more than "product" from their favorite brands. Employees are choosing to work for companies with strong values. Shareholders are more inclined to invest in businesses with outstanding corporate reputations. Quite simply, being socially responsible is not only the right thing to do; it can distinguish a company from its industry peers.[10]

John Ruggie's approach to business and human rights: missing a teachable moment

A crucial issue today for CSR is defining the appropriate responsibility for business when it comes to human rights. Early in the new millennium business leaders were awaiting the results of a UN study outlining the answer to this question. Many scholars involved with ethical and moral questions in business were hopeful that the UN study would focus on making a moral case and not simply a business case. This could have been a teachable moment but unfortunately that moment was lost. Here is the story.

With the advent of the globalization of the economy, multinational firms with operations in developing countries increasingly have been criticized for their human rights records. A subsidiary body of the UN Commission on Human Rights presented in 2003 a draft of a study called the *Norms on Transnational Corporations and Other Business Enterprises*.[11] The key finding of this study was that businesses and states have the *same* human rights responsibilities: "to promote, secure the fulfillment of, respect, ensure respect of, and protect human rights." The UN Draft Norms were an ambitious project that hoped to lay the groundwork for a new international code that would not be voluntary and would eventually become legislation. Needless to say, this controversial position was received with many misgivings in the business community.[12] To equate the roles of states and business in regard to promoting human rights was a principle many in business could not understand. As a result of the controversy, the UN appointed a special representative of the secretary-general (SRSG) on human rights who was charged to develop a coherent position. This assignment was given to Professor John Ruggie, a reputable scholar, advisor to the UN, and now a professor at the Kennedy School of Harvard University.

After more than five years of research and extensive consultation, in March 2011 Ruggie presented what he called the "Protect, Respect and Remedy" Framework along with "Guiding Principles" that provide helpful recommendations for applying the framework.[13] The framework, which some have called "human rights minimalism,"[14] essentially gives business the responsibility to do no harm, to avoid infringing on human rights, and to correct any infringement of rights that is connected to its activity. This duty of business to respect human rights entails acting with due diligence, taking measures to be proactive, and avoiding human rights violations. The state in the framework has the primary responsibility and it includes developing policies, regulation, and adjudication "to protect against human rights violations by business and others and to promote rights." Finally, the framework calls for effective remedies for those who believe they have been victims of human rights abuses.

Ruggie's framework puts limits on the obligations of a business in regard to human rights—namely, the responsibility is do no harm. The framework makes it clear that the state and not business has the positive responsibility to advance human rights. This position gives considerable comfort to business which has had increasing demands by NGOs and other civil society actors to accept new social responsibilities to balance their newly acquired power in the global community. For example, one article several years ago on the HIV/AIDS pandemic in sub-Saharan Africa, where over 25 million people have the disease, cited a critic who "unleashed a verbal broadside against the pharmaceutical companies, and their refusal to provide drugs at cost or, even better, no cost at all."[15] In a similar vein, another article noted that pharmaceutical companies are being "threatened by the National Association of People Living With AIDS if the firms continued to refuse to provide antiretroviral drugs free of charge."[16] The critics based their arguments on the premise that access to life-saving medicines is a human right and that business, in particular pharmaceutical companies, ought to meet this right.

Where there is power there is also responsibility?

In 2000, the UN Economic and Social Council (ECOSOC) stated that "Health is a fundamental human right indispensable for the exercise of other human rights."[17] This right is based on the human dignity of the person and while there is a fairly wide consensus on this right in the global community, there has been wide divergence in how to apportion fairly the responsibilities of meeting the right. Ruggie's framework comes down squarely on the side of the state as the entity charged to protect and advance this and all crucial human rights. While some scholars argue that where there is power, there is also responsibility,[18] Ruggie dismissed the possibility of anchoring the responsibility of a company in its power and resources.

A number of stakeholders have asked whether companies have core human rights responsibilities beyond respecting rights. Some have even advocated that businesses' ability to fulfill rights should translate into a responsibility to do so, particularly where government capacity is limited.

Companies may undertake additional human rights commitments for philanthropic reasons, to protect and promote their brand, or to develop new business opportunities. Operational conditions may dictate additional responsibilities in specific circumstances, while contracts with public authorities for particular projects may require them. In other instances, such as natural disasters or public health emergencies, there may be compelling reasons for any social actor with capacity to contribute temporarily. Such contingent and time-bound actions by some companies in certain situations may be both reasonable and desirable.

However, the proposition that corporate human rights responsibilities as a general rule should be determined by companies' capacity, whether absolute or relative to states, is troubling. On that premise, a large and profitable company operating in a small and poor country could soon find itself called upon to perform ever-expanding social and even governance functions—lacking democratic legitimacy, diminishing the state's incentive to build sustainable capacity, and undermining the company's own economic role and possibly its commercial viability. Indeed, the proposition invites undesirable strategic gaming in any kind of country context.

In contrast, the corporate responsibility to respect human rights exists independently of states' duties or capacity. It constitutes a universally applicable human rights responsibility for all companies, in all situations.[19]

The logic of Ruggie's position is that while it is true that a company with power and resources is able to discharge its social responsibility, power and resources alone are not the source of the responsibility:

"can does not imply ought." My response to Ruggie's position here draws on the logic employed by Leon Sullivan in the apartheid and South Africa case. Sullivan's position was not that "can implies ought" but rather that serious human rights violations imply "ought". The "can" or capability of an actor is one of the criteria for distributing responsibilities among members of the community for remedying the human rights deficit. This responsibility to remedy is a moral obligation and not an optional, philanthropic or charity endeavor.

The Kew Gardens Principle

In the framework, Ruggie never explicitly discusses whether businesses should take on the advancement of crucial human rights when a state is unable or unwilling to do so. For example, did Microsoft have a moral obligation to do something about the education of some of the poor students in developing countries?[20] Did Merck have a moral obligation to do something for *some* of the 25 million people in sub-Saharan Africa with HIV?[21] We know these companies did do something, but were these projects a result of simply voluntary philanthropy or a moral obligation? While Ruggie acknowledges that there are situations "such as natural disasters or public health emergencies" where "any social actor with capacity" might find compelling reasons to assist, this contribution would only be temporary. We never hear from the SRSG that business has a moral obligation to assist in the problems of society, although I will argue that a case might be made using the framework that under certain conditions such a duty is present.

In a study on ethical investing by Simon, Powers and Gunneman,[22] the authors propose that business may, under certain circumstances, have a moral duty to try to advance and protect human rights, even when the business did not in any way cause the problem. To make the case, the authors recount the story of the 1964 stabbing and death of Kitty Genovese in Kew Gardens, New York City, while 38 people looked on. Not one of them took any action to save her life, not even the simple action of calling the police. There was a huge public outcry in the press because people who could have taken some action to try to save her life did nothing. From this incident, the authors formulate what they call the "Kew Gardens Principle." There is a moral obligation to provide assistance in protecting and promoting important human rights when four features are present: 1 critical need; 2 the proximity of potential actors; 3 the capability of those knowing of the problem to assist; and 4 the absence of others who might assist, last resort.

- *Need* is clear when human life is at stake, but in our global economy need can take on a variety of forms in poor and developing countries.
- *Proximity* can be spatial, but at the root it is the awareness—the knowledge of the problem. There is a "network of social expectations" that flow from our various roles, e.g. as a citizen, as a father, and so on, and our responsibility to act flows from these expectations.
- *Capability* follows from the philosophic dictum that "ought" assumes "can." There is no moral responsibility, even in the face of need and proximity, unless there is some action that I am capable of doing to ameliorate the situation.
- *Last resort* is difficult to determine, but often large companies with ample resources know that very few others are able to respond to unique challenges that only they can resolve.

"The Kew Gardens Principle" is an explicit moral or ethical argument that a business has a moral obligation to assist in protecting human rights under certain conditions. Ruggie never employs moral arguments to justify respecting human rights but only relies on making a business case. Respecting human rights will protect a company's reputation, preserve its social license to operate and perhaps enhance its brand. While making the business case for the corporate responsibility to respect human rights is surely important to persuade some leaders, the lack of any explicit moral foundations is puzzling and, in my view, a missed opportunity for a teachable moment. Human rights surely have an instrumental value, but they also have an intrinsic moral value. Advancing human rights can advance business interests but, more importantly, it will advance human interests. Ruggie is very clear that business has a responsibility to respect human rights, especially in cases where governments are unwilling or unable to enforce international and national human rights law, but the justification for this responsibility is "business self interest" (instrumental) rather than a moral argument (intrinsic).

> In addition to compliance with national laws, the baseline responsibility of companies is to respect human rights. Failure to meet this responsibility can subject companies to the courts of public opinion—comprising employees, communities, consumers, civil society, as well as investors—and occasionally to charges in actual courts. Whereas governments define the scope of legal compliance, the broader scope of the responsibility to respect is defined by social

expectations—as part of what is sometimes called a company's social license to operate.[23]

Thus, business should respect human rights in order to meet society's expectations and therefore avoid sanctions or penalties. Some discussion by Ruggie of how society's expectations are largely based on a moral argument would be helpful. A moral argument would focus more on respecting the rights of a person because of the inherent dignity of that person, and not simply because not respecting rights would have adverse consequences for the business. Imagine a case where a company decided that it could take an action and not respect human rights associated with that action but that the public would never know about it, in other words, there is no business case for respecting human rights. Should it not respect the human rights on the basis of a moral case even if there is no business case for doing so?

A moral argument for business advancing rights

In an earlier article, I discussed the question of whether research pharmaceutical companies, which have medicines that can contain HIV/AIDS, have a moral obligation to provide those antiretroviral drugs for at least some of those infected.[24] As indicated above, many NGOs are pressuring multinational pharmaceutical corporations to accept a widening of their role in society based on their immense power and resources, both financial and human. This would clearly be expanding the very purpose of business, giving business part of a state's role—the role to protect and advance human rights. Ruggie's framework would preclude giving business such a *moral duty*, although business would certainly be free to accept such a duty should it decide it is in its interest. In my view, the pharmaceutical/HIV/AIDS case is an early warning signal that there is a paradigm shift underway in formulating the purpose of business in society; hence, it is an insightful case to consider.[25]

It may be helpful to consider the logic of Ruggie's framework in limiting the role of business to respecting human rights, rather than protecting and advancing human rights. Ruggie assumes that while multinational corporations do sometimes assume extraordinary social responsibilities and corporate citizenship duties in developing countries, there is a limit to business's role in society. Individuals (especially wealthy individuals) and nations can and should help provide medicines to all who need them, limited only by their capability. For-profit corporations should see their primary duty as providing good products at a fair price in the context of listening to their many stakeholders. If a pharmaceutical company, for example, depleted its revenue in the process of providing antiretroviral medicines and developing medical clinics for the poor of sub-Saharan Africa, it could not generate the money necessary for research for a cure for HIV/AIDS. Consumers would ultimately pay either by much higher prices or by no new, innovative products or cures (assuming the company survived). To assign the pharmaceutical business the *obligation* of aiding those deprived of antiretroviral medicines and care would undermine the genius of the free enterprise system.

In spite of the compelling logic of the above position, there are a growing number of scholars who argue that with the huge aggregates of money and power under the control of multinational businesses, these organizations *do have moral obligations* as corporate citizens in the global community to assume some responsibility for providing medicines. The very title of the UN program, the Global Compact, points us to the basis of these obligations. All organizations producing goods and services have an implied contract with society. Similar to the argument for the moral and political foundations of the state advanced by Locke, Rousseau, and Hobbes, this approach argues that companies have a duty to be socially responsible and this involves honoring human rights. That being said, the theory does not spell out just what responsibilities are appropriate for multinationals.[26]

Michael A. Santoro, in discussing the duties of multinational firms in the face of human rights violations in China, offers a conceptual framework to assist in the analysis and clarification of the situation. Called a "fair share" theory of human rights, Santoro points us to four factors: "the diversity of actors; the diversity of duties; an allocation of duties among various actors; and principles for a fair allocation."[27] In any human rights problem, there are a number of possible actors, for example, international institutions, nation-states, multinational firms, NGOs and individuals, and each should be allocated a fair share of the duties. The principles proposed for a fair allocation of duties are similar to the Kew Gardens Principle: relationship to those whose rights are violated; the likely effectiveness of the agent in remedying the problem; and the capacity of the agent. Santoro's point is that while companies must do something, they should not be asked to do "more" than they are capable of doing effectively.

Many of our best companies have formulated a philosophy of corporate citizenship and have taken steps to institutionalize this philosophy in their corporate culture. For example, US companies involved with producing antiretroviral medications include Abbott, Bristol-Myers

Squibb, and Merck. Each of these have initiated programs to deliver better health care and treatment, in some limited way, to those suffering HIV/AIDS. I believe these companies correctly perceive that they must do these activities as a matter of moral obligation as corporate citizens and not merely as a matter of philanthropy or as a public relations gesture. From my discussions with some of the companies, I believe they are employing allocation principles similar to Santoro's, largely effectiveness and capacity, and thus are trying to meet a basic moral obligation.[28]

The kind of moral leadership exemplified in Merck's widely discussed Botswana Comprehensive HIV/AIDS Partnership may set a standard of how corporate citizenship can contribute to solving the pandemic. This case may also exemplify how a business can determine its moral obligation to advance human rights.[29]

The framework and the Kew Gardens Principle

The Kew Gardens Principle, as well as the fair share theory discussed above, both assume that respecting and promoting human rights are important for their own sake, as well as for their instrumental value. Most people assume that respect for the law is a basic moral obligation, and thus, it is not debatable that a company follows the law, even if being lawful might lower profits somewhat. Similarly, making the case that respecting human rights is a *moral* obligation for business, that is, that it is done because of the inherent dignity of the person, provides the substantive argument that could help develop consensus in the global community that business ought to advance rights, even if some profit is sacrificed. In the context of a moral argument, the difference between *respecting* human rights and *protecting* and *advancing* those rights pales. For example, in 2012 when Apple was severely criticized for the treatment of workers by its contract supplier in China, Foxconn Technology Group, the critics did not want Apple to leave China or its subcontractor in China (and thus just respect human rights); they wanted Apple to use its leverage to advance and promote human rights. Apple CEO Tim Cook did just that. Cook visited a plant in China and pressed the contract manufacturing group to protect and advance the human rights of its workers by correcting unsafe working conditions, paying a decent wage, avoiding forced labor, and correcting overcrowded dormitories, among other things.[30]

Does Ruggie believe there is a place for the intrinsic moral significance of human rights in the thinking of business? Ruggie's framework implicitly moves toward an ethical or moral basis when it discusses due diligence. Due diligence involves identifying all possible risks to the success of the business, including political, environmental, financial, and even ethical risks. In speaking of due diligence, the framework states:

> Companies routinely conduct due diligence to ensure that a contemplated transaction has no hidden risks. Starting in the 1990s, companies added internal controls for the ongoing management of risks to both the company and stakeholders who could be harmed by its conduct; for example, to prevent employment discrimination, environmental damage or criminal misconduct. Drawing on well-established practices and combining them with what is unique to human rights, the "protect, respect and remedy" framework lays out the basic parameters of human rights due diligence. Because the process is a means for companies to address their responsibility to respect human rights, it must go beyond simply identifying and managing material risks to the company itself to include the risks a company's activities and associated relationships may pose to the rights of affected individuals and communities.[31]

It is important to note that the concern is for risks to the company itself as well as to the rights of affected individuals and community. The report goes on to suggest that companies engage stakeholders and listen to their concerns about their rights. Here rights are being discussed, not because it will save the company money (although it might), but simply because people have a right to have their human rights respected. This may be an opening to developing a moral basis for not only respecting but also protecting and advancing human rights on the part of business. More research and discussion on this and related issues will be helpful.

Theory and practice in the area of human rights: the UN Global Compact

The section has argued that at present the Ruggie framework offers no generally accepted theory that mandates that business take on some of the problems of the wider society as a matter of moral obligation. John Ruggie, in the *Guiding Principles on Business and Human Rights: Implementing the United Nations "Protect, Respect and Remedy" Framework*, postulates that business has a limited obligation. Business must avoid "causing or contributing to adverse human rights impacts through their own activities" and "seek to prevent or mitigate impacts that are directly linked to their operations, products or services by their business relationships." The basic justification of this injunction against "'doing harm' is a business case, that is, that doing harm will have adverse economic impacts on the firm."

Rosabeth Moss Kanter, a highly regarded business scholar, opens her reflections on the new role of business in society as follows: "It's time that beliefs and theories about business catch up with the way great companies operate and how they see their role in the world today."[32] She argues, not too unlike this chapter, for more than a financial logic but for "a social or institutional logic." Unfortunately Ruggie's study is limited to a financial logic and misses the teachable moment to introduce the wider business community to a moral logic involved with CSR. "Institutional logic holds that companies are more than instruments for generating money; they are also vehicles for accomplishing societal purposes and for providing meaningful livelihoods for those who work in them."[33] There is clearly an expanded purpose of business here.

Similar to Rosabeth Moss Kanter's findings, my conclusions as a board member of the United Nations Global Compact Foundation are that many businesses voluntarily commit to projects that support and advance human rights. *The Blueprint for Corporate Sustainability Leadership*[34] reminds signatory companies to the Global Compact that "corporate sustainability is defined as a company's delivery of long-term value in financial, social, environmental and ethical terms." Thus, in this context "to do no harm" means, in ethical terms, to respect human rights *because* they are the rights of a human, even if it might cost some money. As discussed with the Apple case above, from an ethical perspective, the difference between respecting and promoting human rights when it comes to advancing the Millennium Development Goals may not be as great as the Ruggie framework suggests. Does business have a moral responsibility to embrace CSR projects when it can? I stand with those who judge that it does. The next section will offer further discussion of this issue.

The creation of value approach

Chapter 2 discussed the creation of value approach in the work of John Mackey, the Principles for Responsible Management Education (PRME), and that of Michael Porter and Mark Kramer. This section will examine the creation of value approach in more depth and argue that a composite of this strategy is likely to expand CSR in the global economy and bring business's contribution to developing a sustainable global society to scale. The highlights of the Porter and Kramer approach will first be discussed, and then compared and contrasted with the Mackey position. Finally, drawing on elements from all these positions, a composite creation of value approach, an expanded purpose of business, will be suggested.

Michael Porter and Mark Kramer published an insightful article in 2011 titled "Creating Shared Value: How to Reinvent Capitalism—and Unleash a Wave of Innovation and Growth."[35] The basic premise of the article is that "for profit" business can be a most effective organization for solving the problems of society while simultaneously maximizing returns for shareholders, thus the term "shared" value. Some of the highlights of the article that are most congenial with the thesis of this volume include the following:

- The purpose of business. The authors call for a redefinition of the purpose of business from "profit per se" to creating shared value (CSV), capitalism with a social purpose.
- The capitalist system is under siege. There is a remarkable lack of trust in business. "The legitimacy of business has fallen to levels not seen in recent history."
- The interdependence of business and society. "For a business to thrive it needs a successful community and communities need vital businesses to create wealth and jobs. Business must return to the notion that it has broader roles in society, meeting important needs of the community and linking a company's financial success with societal improvement."
- Society has a wide range of unmet needs. The authors list "health, better housing, improved nutrition, help for the aging, greater financial security, and environmental damage."
- Business needs to overcome a short-term focus. The short-term focus found in financial markets and management education must be replaced by a longer time horizon linking business with societal improvement.

Porter and Kramer want to move beyond the typical CSR approach, which they describe as a redistribution approach, and use shared value to create more wealth both for the business and those who need assistance. An excellent example of this win-win strategy is what some companies have done to assist poor farmers who supply their crops to multinationals, for example, cocoa and coffee farmers. The CSR approach is embraced by the fair trade movement and it argues that the farmers should get a higher price for their crops and thus some revenue is redistributed from the company to the farmer. The shared value approach shows how we can create more wealth both for the farmers and the companies. Educating the farmers and introducing technology will produce a better yield and higher-quality crops. Rather than cutting the pie in a new way, the size of the pie is increased to the benefit of all involved. This is not just theory but is actually being done by numerous companies, including Mars and Nestlé.[36] A number of other companies that are successfully practicing CSV are presented in the article.[37]

The traditional CSR is passé according to Porter and Kramer; it is "a feel-good response to external pressure," arising out of charity. "Shared value is not social responsibility, philanthropy, or even sustainability, but a new way to achieve economic success." It is "integral to profit maximization." "Corporate responsibility programs—a reaction to external pressure—have emerged largely to improve firms' reputations and are treated as a necessary expense." "[M]ost companies remain stuck in a 'social responsibility' mind-set in which societal issues are at the periphery, not the core."[38] "Corporate social responsibility is widely perceived as a cost center, not a profit center. In contrast, shared value creation is about new business opportunities that create new markets, improve profitability and strengthen competitive positioning. CSR is about responsibility; CSV is about creating value."[39]

There is no question that CSV has great potential to involve business in the solution of many social and environmental problems. If Porter and Kramer can influence business to take a broader and long-term view, overcoming short-term thinking and focusing on the mutual dependence of business and society, this would be no small achievement in the sustainability journey. On the other hand, to sound the death knell of CSR is to make a serious mistake. One of the major flaws in CSV is one candidly admitted by its proponents, that is, CSV is not the remedy for all societal problems.[40] For CSV to work, companies have to select issues with both economic and social goals, for example, helping poor farmers more effectively produce coffee beans, and then utilize company resources to develop market-based solutions. As we have seen, this has been done by a number of companies and thus a win-win solution is possible with both economic and social value maximized— better long-term profits and a stable source of raw materials for the company and a decent living for the farmer.

The problem is that there are many societal problems that do not lend themselves to a win-win solution. Many companies take on such problems not because they can formulate a business case to justify it but because they develop a moral case—simply put, a company decides that it is the right thing to do. For example, Klaus Leisinger of the Novartis Foundation for Sustainable Development discusses how Novartis distributes medicines for the cure of leprosy patients free of charge to millions of the poorest "because it appears to be the right thing to do."[41] There are times when the right action may not be the one that maximizes profits, just as there are times when in my personal life the right action for me may not be the action that accrues the most benefit to me. That, of course, is what morality and ethics education is all about.[42] While Porter and Kramer's CSV can do much good in the world, it can never replace CSR and its inherent moral compass. This is another way of saying that the basic profit maximization model needs another model to complement and complete it, that the purpose of business must be expanded to include advancing human rights.

Drawing on Adam Smith's first book, *The Theory of Moral Sentiments*, Bill Gates and John Mackey, discussed in Chapter 2, argue that our human nature is so constituted that self-interest is not the only motivation. "Caring for others" is the other deeply rooted drive constitutive of human nature. That insight makes clear that the profit maximization model need not be absolutized for the business system to function effectively. The traditional business logic need not trump the CSR logic (the business ecology model), but rather both logics can complement and complete each other in a new understanding of the purpose of business.

Conclusion

The overarching theme of the chapter is the question of how more companies might be persuaded to participate in CSR so that business might make a substantial contribution to sustainable development. David Vogel argues that the market for virtue largely controls CSR participation and that this market is limited. Thus more government regulation and more pressure from civil society on business is required to increase CSR participation. Bill Frederick, while not denying that more regulation and pressure will facilitate the process, is confident that CSR is motivated not by market rewards but by the wisdom of corporate leadership and that it will expand, slowly but surely. John Mackey and Bill Gates exemplify a new kind of leadership and they espouse a broadened understanding of the purpose of business, employing the dual logic of the market and CSR in the quest for "creation of sustainable value for all stakeholders." John Ruggie, as an unintended consequence of his excellent study on the responsibilities of business in the area of human rights, seems to focus largely on the market logic and neglects any development of the moral case. Michael Porter and Mark Kramer, focusing exclusively on the market logic, argue that all business should be involved in the "creation of shared value," making money while at the same time fashioning a better society through projects in the community that enhance the quality of life.

To be sure, there is truth in all of these perspectives and the best companies employ a combination of these strategies. The next chapter discusses the UN Global Compact and how member companies can contribute to sustainable development through their CSR activities and their CSV endeavors while creating sustainable value for all stakeholders.

Notes

1 David Vogel, *The Market for Virtue: The Potential and Limits of Corporate Social Responsibility* (Washington, DC: Brookings Institution Press, 2005).
2 Vogel, *The Market for Virtue*, 172.
3 Vogel, *The Market for Virtue*, 163.
4 See Joshua Daniel Margolis and James Patrick Walsh, *People and Profits? The Search for a Link Between a Company's Social and Financial Performance* (Mahwah, N.J.: Lawrence Erlbaum, 2001).
5 Robert Reich, *Supercapitalism: The Transformation of Business, Democracy, and Everyday Life* (New York: Vintage, 2008).
6 Bill Frederick, "Vogel and Frederick, Together At Last/ ... Well, Almost" *A Book Review*, www.williamcfrederick.com/articles%20archive/Vogelfrederick. pdf. See also William C. Frederick, *Corporation, Be Good! The Story of Corporate Social Responsibility* (Indianapolis, Ind.: Dog Ear Publishing, 2006).
7 John Elkington, *Cannibals with Forks: The Triple-Bottom Line of 21st Century Business* (New York: Wiley & Sons, 1997).
8 See www.globalreporting.org.
9 Quoted in N. Craig Smith, "Corporate Social Responsibility: Not Whether, But How?" 12, www.facultyresearch.london.edu/docs/03-701.pdf.
10 Quoted in Smith, "Corporate Social Responsibility: Not Whether, But How?" 15.
11 United Nations, *Norms on the Responsibilities of Transnational Corporations and Other Business Enterprises with Regard to Human Rights*, Commission on Human Rights, Sub-Commission on the Promotion and Protection of Human Rights, 55th Session (UN doc. E/CN.4/Sub.2/2003/12/Rev.2).
12 Klaus M. Leisinger, "On Corporate Responsibility for Human Rights," Novartis Foundation; see www.novartisfoundation.org.
13 United Nations, *Guiding Principles on Business and Human Rights: Implementing the United Nations "Protect, Respect and Remedy" Framework*, report of the special representative of the secretary-general on the issue of human rights and transnational corporations and other business enterprises, John Ruggie, Human Rights Council, 17th Session (UN doc. A/ HRD/17/31:2011).

14 For an excellent discussion of the prospect for positive human rights obligations for corporations, see Florian Wettstein, "CSR and the Debate on Business and Human Rights: Bridging the Great Divide," *Business Ethics Quarterly* 22, no. 4 (2012): 739–70.

15 Stephen Lewis, "Silence = Death: AIDS, Africa and Pharmaceuticals," *Toronto Globe and Mail*, 26 January 2001.

16 [author unknown], "Threatened," *Johannesburg Sunday Times*, 2 April 2003.

17 "General Comment No. 14 on Substantive Issues Arising from the Implementation of the International Covenant of Economic, Social and Cultural Rights (ICESCR)," United Nations Economic and Social Council, 2000.

18 Keith Davis and Robert Blomstrom, *Business and its Environment* (New York: McGraw-Hill, 1966).

19 United Nations, *Business and Human Rights: Further Steps Toward the Operationalization of the "Protect, Respect and Remedy" Framework*. Report of the Special Representative of the Secretary-General on the issue of human rights and transnational corporations and other business enterprises, John Ruggie, Human Rights Council (A/HRD/14/27:2010).

20 See www.microsoft.com/citizenship.

21 See www.merck.com.

22 J.G. Simon, C.W. Powers, and J.P. Gunneman, *The Ethical Investor: Universities and Corporate Responsibility* (New Haven, Conn.: Yale University Press, 1972), 22–25.

23 United Nations, *Protect, Respect and Remedy: A Framework for Business and Human Rights*, report of the special representative of the secretary-general on the issue of human rights and transnational corporations and other business enterprises, John Ruggie, Human Rights Council (UN doc. A/HRC/8/5:2008). For discussion of this point, see Wesley Cragg, "Ethics, Enlightened Self-Interest, the Corporate Responsibility to Respect Human Rights: A Critical Look at the Justificatory Foundations of the UN Framework," *Business Ethics Quarterly* 22, no. 1 (2012): 9–36.

24 Oliver F. Williams, "The UN Global Compact: The Challenge and the Promise," *Business Ethics Quarterly* 14, no. 4 (2004): 755–74.

25 Smith, "Corporate Social Responsibility: Not Whether, But How?" 8–11.

26 For an excellent discussion of these issues, see Thomas Donaldson, *The Ethics of International Business* (Oxford: Oxford University Press, 1989).

27 Michael A. Santoro, "Engagement with Integrity: What We Should Expect Multinational Firms to Do About Human Rights in China," *Business and the Contemporary World* 10, no. 1 (1998): 25–54.

28 The previous four paragraphs follow closely from an earlier article. See Williams, "The UN Global Compact: The Challenge and the Promise," 755–74.

29 See www.achap.org.

30 Charles Duhigg and Steven Greenhouse, "Electronic Giant Vowing Reforms in China Plants," *The New York Times*, 29 March 2012.

31 United Nations, *Business and Human Rights: Further Steps* ... , John Ruggie, Human Rights Council (UN doc. A/HRC/14/27:2010).

32 Rosabeth Moss Kanter, "How Great Companies Think Differently," *Harvard Business Review* 89, no. 11 (2011): 68.

33 Moss Kanter, "How Great Companies Think Differently," 68.

34 UN Global Compact, *The Blueprint for Corporate Sustainability Leadership*, www.unglobalcompact.org/docs/news_events/8.1/Blueprint.pdf.
35 Michael E. Porter and Mark R. Kramer, "Creating Shared Value: How to Reinvent Capitalism—and Unleash a Wave of Innovation and Growth," *Harvard Business Review* 89 nos. 1 and 2 (2011): 1–17.
36 The Nestlé case is discussed in Lisa Newton and John Bee, "Creating Shared Value: Nestlé S.A. in Developing Nations," in *Peace Through Commerce: Responsible Corporate Citizenship and the Ideals of the United Nations Global Compact*, ed. Oliver F. Williams (Notre Dame, Ind.: University of Notre Dame Press, 2008), 329–35.
37 Companies participating in CSV cited by the authors include Intel, IBM, GE, WaterHealth International, Marks & Spencer, Coca-Cola, Dow Chemical, Nestlé, Kindle, Hindustan Unilever, and Johnson & Johnson.
38 Above quotes are from Porter and Kramer, "Creating Shared Value," 4–5, 15–17.
39 Mark Kramer, "A Response to 'Shared Value': CSR Re-branded?" realizedworth.posterous.com/michael-porter-mark-kramer-want-you-to-abando.
40 Porter and Kramer, "Creating Shared Value," 17.
41 Klaus M. Leisinger, "Stretching the Limits of Corporate Responsibility," in *Peace Through Commerce: Responsible Corporate Citizenship and the Ideals of the United Nations Global Compact*, ed. Oliver F. Williams (Notre Dame, Ind.: University of Notre Dame Press, 2008), 223.
42 For a good text on business ethics see Manuel G. Velasquez, *Business Ethics: Concepts and Cases* (Upper Saddle River, N.J.: Pearson Prentice Hall, 2006).

4 Corporate social responsibility as an instrument of global governance

The UN Global Compact

- **Global norms of conduct: an idea whose time has come**
- **The UN Global Compact: its history and its promise**
- **Is the UN Global Compact the final answer?**
- **Conclusion: the Global Compact as a process to create a sustainable future**

One of the issues that emerged with the globalization of the economy is the lack of common agreement on the appropriate norms that should guide business, especially in developing countries. Is a multinational company responsible for human rights violations of its subcontractors? What are appropriate norms for guiding a company's environmental policy in a country where there is no legal framework, at least in practice? One new initiative to promote and enhance the development of more just norms in developing countries is the United Nations Global Compact (UNGC). Founded in 2000 by the then UN Secretary-General Kofi Annan, the Global Compact is intended to increase and diffuse the benefits of global economic development through voluntary corporate policies and programs. By promoting human rights and labor rights, enhancing care for the environment and encouraging anticorruption measures, the 10 principles of the Global Compact are designed to enable more peaceful societies. In addition to integrating the 10 principles into their strategic plan, companies are also asked to take on projects that advance UN goals. Initially comprising several dozen companies, the compact as of 2013 had over 7,000 businesses and 1,000 nongovernmental organizations (NGOs) in 135 countries. The objective is to emphasize the moral purpose of business, with member companies setting a high moral tone throughout the world. Ban Ki-moon, secretary-general of the UN, in 2007 expressed the mission well: "Business practices rooted in universal values can bring social and economic gains."

Part of the mission of the Global Compact is to foster the growth of humane values in the global society. The underlying insight is that without the values embedded in the compact—for example, trust, fairness, integrity, and respect for people—global capitalism would eventually lose legitimacy in the wider society. As discussed in Chapter 2, there is much evidence from surveys on trust that people are increasingly losing trust in business. Public trust in business institutions and leadership is at a low level. When people perceive that business is not only seeking its private good but also the common good, and that this is embodied in a mission statement and a widened purpose and activity, there is a slow retrieval of trust in business. This retrieval of trust is manifest in the response to some of the endeavors of signatory companies of the Global Compact. There is a growing awareness by multinational companies that global business is only possible in a world where basic ethical principles are assumed. As discussed below, some evidence for this moral sensitivity of multinational companies is seen in the formation of the Caux Principles, a set of moral ideals not too unlike the compact subscribed to by a number of prominent global companies. Founded in 1986, the Caux Principles do not have the visibility, global reach and convening power with many stakeholders that accrue under the umbrella of the United Nations, but they do represent a significant attempt by companies to accent the moral purpose of business. Largely because of the UN sponsorship, I argue that the compact has the potential to be a more effective vehicle than Caux could be.

The first three chapters of the book tell of the evolution of the meaning of the term "corporate social responsibility" (CSR), and how we are in the midst of a major paradigm shift in our understanding of the purpose of business. For many companies this transition came with struggles and conflict with civil society, as the South Africa and apartheid case demonstrates. Other companies with unusually precocious leadership charted a new destiny for business with a voluntary global ethic that suited the times and with an expanded purpose of business— namely, creating sustainable value for all stakeholders. To develop a global consensus on this new understanding, however, is a work in progress and is the subject of this chapter.

There is little doubt that globalization hastened if not caused this paradigm shift. Globalization refers to the integration of international economic activity at a level unheard of not too long ago. Not only does it involve unparalleled movements of capital but also of goods and services, technologies, and people. The first section of this chapter discusses how globalization resulted in a call for a new global ethic. A discussion follows of the UN Global Compact and how it might meet the needs of the time. The next section focuses on the strengths and weaknesses of the Global Compact and finally the conclusion suggests that the compact, for all its shortcomings, is our best hope.

Global norms of conduct: an idea whose time has come

In the 1990s with the huge expansion of the global economy and out-sourcing into poor developing countries, there was much public attention and controversy around the issues of sweatshops and child labor. The focus of much of the public controversy was on Nike and whether the company had a responsibility for the inhumane practices of its subcontractors. Nike at first claimed no responsibility for the conduct of its suppliers and contractors, as these were independent and not owned by the multinational. After a consumer boycott, Nike later changed its position, formulated a code of conduct for suppliers, and became a model employer.[1] For purposes of this study, the important point to note is that because of the Nike case and other similar ones there was a growing concern about globalization in the late 1990s.

Globalization is perceived as being both a threat and a promise. The promise is seen in the rising prosperity experienced by many in rich and poor countries alike in the aftermath of international linkages.[2] The threat is the growing perception, by nations and by individuals, that no longer can we control our way of life. Whether it is corporate downsizing, take-overs, rapid withdrawal of finances, bankruptcies, human rights abuses, or the loss of jobs, the pace of change and the disruption of communities is very troubling to many. Joseph Schumpeter's "Creative Destruction," described so well in his 1940 work, *Capitalism, Socialism and Democracy*, is a double-edged sword that cries out for a humane resolution.[3]

Business, as one of the major institutions of society, was in the fore-front of this challenge. In the late 1990s there was a growing call for global ethics. From various parts of the world, proposals were emerging for a new global code of conduct. For example, the Caux Round Table Principles are largely the work of Japanese, European and US business leaders.[4] The CERES Principles are an attempt to protect the worldwide environment.[5] There is an ever-increasing concern that human rights in developing countries be promoted and protected, highlighted in the code for the apparel industry, the US White House Apparel Industry Code of Conduct.[6] In South Africa, there were the famous Sullivan Principles[7] and in Northern Ireland there were the Macbride Principles.[8]

The basic premise is that good ethics mean good business. Business needs predictability in order to thrive and ethics codes ensure that predictability has a chance. A global ethic is a requirement of our new situation of the shrinking borders of our world, compressing peoples, cultures and economies. Technology and the internet has hastened the arrival of our global village and the challenge to fashion a humane village is one that remains for our time.

The nature of globalization is such that the role of the firm was being redefined as well as the role of national and global institutions. The challenge requires that business define its ethical responsibility with global standards just as it defines product, production and employee standards. With this new relationship between business and society aborning, some were suggesting the need for an international treaty between governments and multinational business to clarify expectations and standards. Following the practice of the US Department of State in producing an Annual Report on Human Rights Practices of countries, some suggested that NGOs author a report describing the behavior of the top 500 multinational companies in the human rights area.

In the 1990s there were anti-corruption codes put forward by the major international governmental and nongovernmental organizations. The Organisation for Economic Co-operation and Development (OECD), the Organization of American States (OAS), the European Union (EU), the World Trade Organization (WTO), the World Bank, the UN Commission on Transnational Corporations (UNCTC), the International Chamber of Commerce, and Transparency International (TI) are all international instruments working effectively to combat corruption. Significant progress has been made and many are optimistic.[9]

For most business leaders, the global ethic that held the most promise, largely because it was formulated by the business community, was Caux Round Table's Principles for Business. In 1986 a group of senior business executives from Japan, Europe, and North America began meeting annually in Caux, Switzerland to discuss measures to lessen trade tensions. These discussions led to further meetings about ethical issues and finally, in 1994, to the adoption of the Caux Principles for Business. Many are champions of the Caux Principles not only because they are a set of ethical standards that hold across cultures but also because they are advocated and advanced by business leaders themselves rather than NGOs or others. The principles address the responsibilities of managers and companies from a stakeholder perspective and include all the elements that a company may want to include in its own code of conduct.

A crucial issue in any code formulation is how to develop accountability structures—that is, how to develop effective monitoring. A code that may be a model for its monitoring provisions is the US White House Apparel Partnership Workplace Code of Conduct and Principle Monitoring. The document is the fruit of a presidential task force formed in 1996 after the outcry that followed revelations that a line of clothing bearing the name of the US TV talk-show host Kathie Lee Gifford was made in sweatshops in Central America and New York.

Composed of human rights groups and apparel manufacturers, the 18-member task force met for more than two years before 13 of the members finally agreed to go forward with the code in November 1998. Apparel manufacturers on the task force agreeing were: Liz Claiborne, Nike, Reebok, Phillips Van Heusen, L.L. Bean, Patagonia, Nicole Miller, and Kathie Lee Gifford. The human rights organizations signing off on the code included: Business for Social Responsibility, the Lawyers Committee for Human Rights, the National Consumers League, the International Labor Rights Fund and Robert F. Kennedy Memorial Center for Human Rights.

This anti-sweatshop code has a mechanism for independent monitoring to avoid child labor, forced overtime, sexual harassment, unsafe working conditions and a host of other problems often found in the apparel manufacturing industry, especially in emerging nations.

Slowly but surely, a global ethic was catching on in the business community. This surely was an idea whose time had come.

In 2000 I published a book titled *Global Codes of Conduct: An Idea Whose Time Has Come*, which included essays by many of the major scholars in the area as well as appendices with most of the major codes contending for the global ethic.[10] In my view, the Caux Principles had the best chance of gaining legitimacy in the global business community, given that their formulation involved significant business leaders and also that they were an international endeavor from the start. All that changed when in January 1999, the then secretary-general of the United Nations, Kofi Annan, spoke to the World Economic Forum in Davos, Switzerland, about the need for a new Global Compact for business. The next section will discuss this development.

The UN Global Compact: its history and its promise

In the late 1990s many followers of the world scene were convinced that the globalized world needed to gain consensus on new forms of global governance. The regulatory authority of the nation-state was eroded with the growing power of multinational business. Applying international or national law to companies operating in dozens of countries had little prospect for success. In fact, as evidenced in the

Nike case, global governance was often facilitated by civil society actors bringing moral pressure on business, and as we saw with the Caux Principles in the previous section, business was partnering with NGOs and academics to formulate global norms for its operations. Business was taking on the character of a political actor not only in formulating new rules of conduct for itself but also in accepting new responsibilities, for example, in protecting workers' rights, participating in the fight over HIV/AIDS, and advancing education in poor areas. Yet the lingering problem remained that for every Nike that transformed itself from an amoral company to a leading light, there were hundreds of companies that were unaware of their responsibilities in the area of human rights as well as the social and environmental issues in developing countries. It was in this context that Kofi Annan gave his address at Davos in 1999.

The basic proposal of Annan, that business and the United Nations join together to promulgate a "global compact of shared values and principles, to give a human face to the global market," was met with widespread approval in the business community.[11] When the secretary-general, in 2000, first promulgated the Global Compact, he had a clear vision of the problem, but only a broad outline of the solution. The problem was that globalization of markets, while it created vast amounts of new wealth, did not distribute this new wealth very well. Millions of people in India and China were lifted out of poverty, but many people in the world were victims rather than beneficiaries of this new engine of wealth creation. Whether it be blue-collar workers who lost lucrative jobs on auto assembly lines in Detroit, populations of major cities in China that lost clean air to breathe or poor peasants who were subjected to sweatshop conditions in Asia and Latin America, increasing discontent was in the air. In former times of great economic volatility, nation-states took measures that restored social harmony and political stability.

For example, the Great Depression of some 75 years ago was the birthplace of the social safety net, evolving into such programs as social security, medical benefits, unemployment insurance, food stamps and so on. The problems today are global in scope and even where nation-states might be willing or able to regulate, they are reluctant to do so for fear of losing new investment to nations with less stringent regulations. The race to the bottom is a fact of life in developing countries.

Kofi Annan saw clearly that if globalization and its ability to create massive wealth was to continue, there must be a set of ideals that would guide business and ensure that the legitimate concerns of all, especially the least advantaged, were not neglected. This set of ideals, what has become known as the Global Compact, consists of 10 principles. Over 7,000 businesses throughout the world have already signed on as participants (as of 30 April 2013 there were over 7,000 business participants and 3,000 civil society signatories).

The 10 principles of the Global Compact focus on human rights, labor rights, concern for the environment and corruption, and are taken directly from commitments made by governments through the UN: the Universal Declaration of Human Rights (1948); the Rio Declaration on Environment and Development (1992); the International Labor Organization's Fundamental Principles and Rights at Work (1998); and the UN Convention Against Corruption (2003). The text of the 10 principles is as follows:

The Ten Principles of the United Nations Global Compact
The Global Compact asks companies to embrace, support and enact, within their sphere of influence, a set of core values in the areas of human rights, labor standards, the environment and anti-corruption.

Human Rights
Principle 1   Businesses should support and respect the protection of internationally proclaimed human rights; and
Principle 2   make sure that they are not complicit in human rights abuses.

Labor
Principle 3   Businesses should uphold the freedom of association and the effective recognition of the right to collective bargaining;
Principle 4   the elimination of all forms of forced and compulsory labor;
Principle 5   the effective abolition of child labor; and
Principle 6   the elimination of discrimination in respect of employment and occupation.

Environment
Principle 7   Businesses should support a precautionary approach to environmental challenges;
Principle 8   undertake initiatives to promote greater environmental responsibility; and
Principle 9   encourage the development and diffusion of environmentally friendly technologies.

Anti-Corruption
Principle 10   Businesses should work against corruption in all its forms, including extortion and bribery.

In addition to making the principles an integral part of the business strategy and corporate culture, a company is asked to engage in partnerships to advance broader development goals (e.g., The Sustainable Development Goals of the UN).[12]

The Global Compact was designed as a voluntary initiative. A company subscribing to the Principles is invited to make a clear statement of support and must include some references in its annual report or other public documents on the progress it is making on internalizing the principles within its operations. This Communication on Progress (COP) must also be submitted to be posted on the Global Compact website.[13] Failure to submit a COP within two years of becoming a signatory to the compact (and subsequently every year) will result in being delisted. As of July 2013, over 4,000 companies had been removed from the list of participants for failure to communicate progress.

Scholars have suggested that corporate responsibility initiatives may be categorized as one of four different types: principle-based initiatives, certification initiatives, reporting initiatives, and process-based initiatives.[14] Certification initiatives, for example, Social Accountability 8000,[15] have auditing and verification procedures. Reporting initiatives are best represented by the Global Reporting Initiative (GRI), a series of some 70 suggested questions, to assist in preparing a sustainability report about the environmental, social and governance (ESG) issues.[16] Process-based initiatives are best represented by the ISO 26000, an outline of a process to enable businesses to integrate CSR into the business plan.[17] Principle-based initiatives are best represented by the Caux Principles, the UN Global Compact, and the OECD Guidelines for Multinational Enterprises. Principle-based initiatives are a set of ideals, general in nature, that members of an organization are expected to follow; these norms have no explicit enforcement mechanism. I find the UN Global Compact, a principle-based initiative, the one that is most likely to succeed in garnering the global consensus required to establish the legitimacy of the norms. The UN has already established itself as legitimate in the eyes of many in the global community and the universal norms of the Global Compact are at the heart of the UN, having been based on UN documents.

The unique mission of the compact is to foster the growth of humane values in the *global* society, a challenge heretofore managed by nation-states for their own domestic situation. To advance the 10 principles, the Global Compact has established over 100 country and regional networks where dialogue, learning and projects are carried forward in a local context. Kofi Annan, former secretary-general, expressed it well: "Let us choose to unite the power of markets within the authority of universal ideals. Let us choose to reconcile the creative forces of private entrepreneurship with the needs of the disadvantaged and the requirements of future generations."

Developing a consensus on global ethical norms: the major challenge

As indicated earlier, I am convinced that the Global Compact is the best initiative that can meet the major challenge posed by globalization: developing a consensus on global ethical norms. The United Nations with its visibility, global reach, universality, neutrality and convening power is considered legitimate in our world today and with the local networks of the UNGC operating almost everywhere, there are channels of communication readily available. Through the process of persuasion, discussion and arguing about practices, e.g. sweatshops, the norms and values that enable global governance are internalized; major players are "socialized" and the voluntary compliance of the UNGC shapes the new CSR agenda.[18] There is a growing recognition that the CSR agenda of the UNGC is a legitimate one; as a visiting professor in Asia for the 2012–13 academic year, I have been especially impressed by many of the Global Compact members in China where there is a relatively new UNGC local network, and where the CSR agenda has taken hold. The normative worth of the UN, specifically the universal values embodied in the 10 principles of the UNGC, is widely accepted in Asia.

The Global Compact China Network, with over 300 companies, consists of Chinese state-owned companies, private companies and multinationals in China. At a 2011 meeting:

> Peng Huagang, Director General of the Research Bureau of the Chinese State Assets Supervision and Administration Commission of the State Council (SASAC) expressed emphasis on corporate responsibility among its member companies and its support of the Global Compact. "The Global Compact China Network will facilitate the communication and collaboration between Chinese and foreign companies, helping Chinese companies to make a greater contribution to the UN MDGs [Millennium Development Goals]. I sincerely wish that the Global Compact China Network will play a greater role to enhance corporate social responsibility and international collaboration."[19]

The governance of the UNGC initially comprised the secretary-general and a multi-stakeholder advisory council but in 2005 a new framework was established which reflected both the rapid expansion of the compact and its unique mission. Following a network-based governance model, authority is now decentralized among five entities: the UNGC Board (appointed by the UN secretary-general), the UNGC Office, the UN Inter-Agency Team,[20] the Local Networks and the Government Donor Group (the 13 countries that have voluntarily funded the UNGC).[21] Two regular meetings are also involved in governance: the Annual Local Networks Forum and the triennial Global Compact Leaders' Summit. This arrangement has fostered legitimacy by involving both public and private actors in crucial decisions and encouraging ownership by a wide variety of stakeholders. In 2006, the UNGC established a not-for-profit foundation [501(c)(3)] under New York State law and now asks all companies to contribute. This funding helps to provide materials to enhance global corporate sustainability, to assist local networks, and to foster participation at events of the UNCG. In a memorandum of understanding (MOU) between the foundation and the UN, the foundation's main functions include fundraising to support the work of the UNGC and "promotion and advocacy of the Global Compact and its principles."[22] The website of the foundation lists all the contributors to the foundation as well as how the funds were spent.

Additional reasons for advocating for the Global Compact

To be sure, there is a business case for corporate responsibility and the work of the compact. Not only does following the principles have a high likelihood of saving the company money by avoiding costly litigation but it also enhances reputation capital, builds brands, enables a company to attract and retain valuable employees, develops trust, and so on. In addition, creating sustainable value in a company by attending to ESG performance is increasingly rewarded by the investment community. The Global Compact is one of the factors advancing the trend toward a broadening of the criteria by which the market assesses the performance of companies. This broadening of criteria is reflected in two movements inspired by the Global Compact, one in the investment community and one in higher education. The Principles for Responsible Investment (PRI) is a credo subscribed to by over 1,000 leading investment managers throughout the world and currently has some US$30 trillion of assets under its management. The principles of the PRI, launched in 2006, are as follows:

> As institutional investors, we have a duty to act in the best long-term interests of our beneficiaries. In this fiduciary role, we believe

that environmental, social, and corporate governance (ESG) issues can affect the performance of investment portfolios (to varying degrees across companies, sectors, regions, asset classes and through time). We also recognize that applying these Principles may better align investors with broader objectives of society. Therefore, where consistent with our fiduciary responsibilities, we commit to the following:

- We will incorporate ESG issues into investment analysis and decision-making processes.
- We will be active owners and incorporate ESG issues into our ownership policies and practices.
- We will seek appropriate disclosure on ESG issues by the entities in which we invest.
- We will promote acceptance and implementation of the Principles within the investment industry.
- We will work together to enhance our effectiveness in implementing the Principles.
- We will each report on our activities and progress towards implementing the Principles.[23]

The Principles for Responsible Management Education (PRME)[24] is a code for business schools reflecting the need to educate future business leaders with this new, broadened vision. Almost 500 business schools in nearly 80 countries have already subscribed to this new initiative (see Chapter 2).

While many companies find the business case for the Global Compact compelling, it is the moral case that has the interest of some leading NGOs and critics of globalization. These critics are concerned that in developing countries where there is no enforced statutory framework to protect workers and the environment, multinational corporations are acting unethically with impunity. Many NGOs have risen to the occasion and mobilized public opinion about the need for some global standards. As for the Global Compact, there is evidence that businesses are walking the talk. The 2011 Global Compact Implementation Survey sent to all UNGC companies showed that: 63 percent of the companies considered supplier adherence to sustainability principles; smaller companies showed gains in key areas (human rights, anti-corruption, subsidiaries and supplier engagement); 75 percent of the companies are involved in projects to advance UN goals; and a majority of companies indicated involvement in partnership projects.[25]

The 10 principles of the Global Compact were given added force by the UN MDGs, a blueprint for action agreed to by all the countries of the world as well as leading development institutions. With the target date of 2015 for completion, the eight MDGs are: 1 eradicate extreme poverty and hunger; 2 achieve universal primary education; 3 promote gender equality and empower women; 4 reduce child mortality; 5 improve maternal health; 6 combat HIV/AIDS, malaria and other diseases; 7 ensure environmental sustainability; and 8 develop a global partnership for development. Facilitated by the Global Compact Office, commitment to these ideals has brought businesses into new collaborative relationships with NGOs throughout the world. The Global Compact website offers many examples of companies working to eradicate poverty and advance the MDGs.[26] In 2016, upon reaching the target date of the MDGs, the UN in close collaboration with the UNGC, will release the Sustainable Development Goals (SDGs) and the post-2015 agenda. The SDGs will continue the focus on eradicating poverty and will include the rule of law, jobs, food, water and energy, social issues (e.g. the Women's Empowerment Principles), health, and financial reform.

What about the critics of the Global Compact?

From the start, there have been some strident critics of the UNGC.[27] One important set of critics is simply not convinced that economic globalization is a good idea. Another group believes that without some required certification process that companies are walking the talk, business will use the UNGC as a cover story, "bluewash" as it is called (powder blue is the UN color). A third group of critics is within the UN itself and fears that business may become too influential in the United Nations. Each group will be considered briefly.

An important group of critics does not believe that economic globalization, as it is presently conceived, will ever bring authentic development to the poor, even if the principles of the compact were implemented.[28] Accountability for this sort of critic would involve carefully assessing whether the poor and developing nations are indeed better off with economic globalization. They are angry that Kofi Annan with his Global Compact and its voluntary nature has assumed the answer. In the final analysis, this school of thought sees the only answer to the plight of the poor as a radical change, "a binding legal framework for the transnational behavior of business in the human rights, environmental and labor realms."[29]

A 20 July 2000 letter from prominent scholars and NGO leaders to UN Secretary-General Kofi Annan summarizes this objection.

> We recognize that corporate-driven globalization has significant support among governments and business. However, that support

is far from universal. Your support for this ideology, as official UN policy, has the effect of delegitimizing the work and aspirations of those sectors that believe that an unregulated market is incompatible with equity and environmental sustainability ... Many do not agree with the assumption of the Global Compact that globalization in its current form can be made sustainable and equitable, even if accompanied by the implementation of standards for human rights, labor, and the environment ... We are well aware that many corporations would like nothing better than to wrap themselves in the flag of the United Nations in order to "bluewash" their public image, while at the same time avoiding significant changes to their behavior ... Without monitoring, the public will be no better able to assess the behavior, as opposed to the rhetoric, of corporations.[30]

It is well beyond the bounds of this study to make some final judgment on the merits of the contemporary practice of economic globalization, but I do submit that there is a convergence in the vision of the globalization critics and the compact. Both are trying to retrieve the notion that there is a moral purpose of business and not only in wealth creation but also in its distribution.

One way to view the compact is as an attempt to revive the moral underpinnings of the economy that were assumed by Adam Smith. In *An Inquiry into the Nature and Causes of the Wealth of Nations* (*The Wealth of Nations*), Smith sought to understand why some nations were wealthier than others. Part of his answer was that nations that encouraged free competitive markets were wealthier. In a curious kind of way, in the context of the economy, when *each person pursues his or her self-interest the common good is enhanced* and all are wealthier. Given competition, the baker bakes the very best bread possible and sells it at the lowest price feasible that will enable him to have the resources to buy what he wants. Although motivated by self-interest, the result is that the community has good bread at a reasonable cost. Thus Smith showed how economic self-interest was beneficial for the community.[31]

In my view, however, the crucial point in Smith's analysis is his assumption in *The Wealth of Nations* that is quite explicit in his *The Theory of Moral Sentiments*: The "self-interest" of business people would be shaped by moral forces in the community so that self-interest would not always degenerate into greed and selfishness.[32] Wealth creation enabled and sustained a humane community when it was practiced by virtuous people. This, of course, was the point that was made in discussing the business philosophy of John Mackey in Chapter 2.

My argument is that Smith assumed that an acquisitive economy existed in the context of a moral community that would ensure that single-minded focus on making money would not persist.[33] Yet it is precisely this challenge of fostering the growth of humane values in the *global* society, a challenge heretofore managed by nation-states for their own domestic situation, that marks the unique mission of the Global Compact. The argument made by Global Compact officials is that unless the moral purpose of business is retrieved, economic globalization is doomed to failure.

> It is precisely because a backlash to globalization would represent a historically unmatched threat to economic prosperity and peace that the Global Compact urges international business leaders to take reasonable steps to secure the emerging values of global civil society in exchange for a commitment on the part of the United Nations to market openness.[34]

Globalization critics see little value in the compact unless "the emerging values of global civil society" are somehow mandated by a worldwide legal framework. The compact, seeing little prospect for worldwide legal statutes, advances a vision of the moral purpose of business that relies on transparency and the interest companies have in maintaining their good reputation as the ultimate sanction.

A second group of critics focuses on the fact that a company reporting annually on its progress in advancing the 10 principles of the UNGC, in what is called its COP report, is not required to have the report certified or audited. Critics continue to call for some performance standards and verification procedures. Prakash Sethi writes: "The Global Compact ... provides a venue for opportunistic companies to make grandiose statements of corporate citizenship without worrying about being called to account for their actions."[35] Compact officials respond that this criticism misses the point. "The Global Compact is not designed as a code of conduct. Rather it is a means to serve as a (frame) of reference to stimulate best practices and to bring about convergence around universally shared values."[36] At this stage, the goal is to gain consensus on the moral purpose of business and to include the substance of the principles as a part of business strategy and operations. Since companies will include a discussion of their compact-related activities in their annual reports, the power of public transparency and the watchdog role of the media and NGOs serve as an accountability structure. What compact advocates have in mind is that when actual business practice falls short of ethical standards, public criticism is a good corrective. For example, Lynn Sharp Paine, in an insightful study of the merging of social and financial imperatives, discusses how Royal Dutch/Shell made a major change in policy and practice after strident criticism of its activities in Nigeria.[37] Although Shell had serious problems in 2004 with top management overstating oil reserves, the company is still considered by many to be a leader in promoting and protecting the rights of workers and communities. Yet even with this role of the press and activist groups, while the compact is a noble endeavor, unless the participating companies are involved in some sort of independent monitoring and verification system, corporate critics (even those in the moderate camp) may never acknowledge its legitimacy.

Of course, one premise of the compact is that there will always be NGOs, activists, social investors and others who will be on the scene to pressure firms and the Global Compact to be better corporate citizens. There is a growing realization that NGOs or organizations of civil society play an important role in such a dialogue, for their focus is properly the common good—the culture of civility, health, environmental protection, and so on. This is certainly not to say that NGOs are always above reproach, for they too need accountability structures. In economic terms, NGOs focus on overcoming the negative externalities of business. Major NGOs, including Amnesty International, Human Rights First, The Nature Conservancy, Global Witness, and Transparency International are participating in the deliberations of the compact. The International Confederation of Free Trade Unions, Business Associations, and Academic and Public Policy Institutions have joined the compact and are active participants.[38]

A third group of critics of the UNGC is within the UN itself. Historically the UN did not have a close relationship with the private sector and in the 1960s this was amplified as many developing countries moved away from their colonial masters and became independent. The UN served as countervailing power for developing countries that understood multinational companies to be part of the problem of muted economic and human development and certainly not the solution. All this began to change in the 1990s and was accelerated with the election of Kofi Annan as secretary-general. There were a number of moves to enhance cooperation between UN institutions and the business world.

Georg Kell, the very talented executive director of the UNGC since its founding in 2000, wrote an insightful piece on the history and development of the project.[39] As indicated in the 20 July 2000 letter cited above, some NGO and academic leaders strongly disagreed that globalization could be rendered more helpful to the poor and many in the UN were opposed to Kofi Annan taking a strong stand for the Global Compact. In the face of some opposition within the UN, Annan courageously decided to make a plea for a closer relationship between business and the UN at his January 1999 address before the World Economic Forum at Davos. Business leaders were enthusiastic about closer cooperation with the UN not only because the UN supported public goods essential for world trade (e.g. security, monetary rules and infrastructure improvement), but perhaps more importantly because the UN had a consensus on human rights and the implications for labor, the environment and corruption. It is important to note that when Annan officially launched the Global Compact in 2000 it did not have a mandate from the member states of the General Assembly. Only in 2007 did the General Assembly finally allow the Global Compact to be called the UN Global Compact, signaling that the pet project of the secretary-general was now a UN project.

The challenge in the early years of the compact was to get enough UN employees up to speed on how to work with business. If business was to take action to advance UN goals, a tenet of the UNGC, UN personnel had to have the knowledge and skills to facilitate this task. An inter-agency working group was formed in the UN to have developed personnel in the various UN agencies and has been relatively successful.

While no one would claim that all UN officials are today passionate advocates of the UNGC, Kell argues that many who were skeptics early in the game are now "strong supporters."[40] With the election of Ban Ki-moon as secretary-general in 2006, the UN had a talented leader who believed in the future of UN-business partnerships and the importance of the UNGC. One major challenge that remains for the UN leadership is to ensure that the principles of the Global Compact are embedded in the UN itself: Does it practice what it preaches? This too is a work in progress.

Is the UN Global Compact the final answer?

To be sure, there is no final answer. If the purpose of business is to create sustainable value for all stakeholders, and if the UN Global Compact is the best available way to bring businesses together for this common journey, then it is a good answer until we find a better one. There is much evidence that sustainable value, although incremental, is largely underway because of the Global Compact. Chapter 5 will present several examples of how companies are operationalizing the universal values of the compact in their practice. For now, it may be helpful to address those critics who see the only answer as a worldwide legal framework (hard law) rather than a set of voluntary principles (soft law).

Hard law is understood as binding and enforceable while soft law is legally non-binding. Typically soft law appears in the form of guidelines, resolutions or principles. The Global Compact is considered soft law but like most soft law, there are penalties for joining the UNGC and then not complying, for example, by not submitting a COP. As indicated earlier, over 4,000 businesses have been expelled for not complying—that is, not submitting the required COP.

Scholars have noted that hard law seldom just appears on the scene but rather has a history and usually follows when norms, soft laws and customs that are thought to be important by society are flagrantly violated.[41] For example, the US Foreign Corrupt Practices Act (FCPA) passed in 1976 by the Congress outlawed bribery of foreign government officials and other corrupt practices in business after the public was outraged by a huge bribe Lockheed paid to Japanese officials to obtain a large order of aircraft. There long had been a custom, a norm, and a soft law in the industry against bribery but it took egregious violation of soft law to energize the evolution to hard law. The FCPA is an unusual case because it was one of the major drivers of global soft law on bribery, the 1997 OECD Convention on Anti-Bribery. This soft law, in turn, influenced the United States to amend the FCPA to include the new features found in the OECD Convention, resulting in the 1998 International Anti-Bribery Act (soft law becoming hard law).

There are a number of examples where it becomes clear that soft law cannot achieve the desired results and thus society influences the governing body to move to hard law with sanctions. This is clear in the US Sarbanes Oxley legislation which requires that companies keep detailed records supporting their financial statements and has severe penalties for senior officers when financial statements are found fraudulent. Before Enron and WorldCom this was standard practice (soft law); now it is standard practice with tough enforceable sanctions (hard law).

All of this discussion on hard and soft law is by way of noting that in much of the world there have not been norms, customs and soft laws that guide business. A significant value of the UN Global Compact is to highlight the normative dimension, the universal values of the UN and bring them into the strategic plan of a business. Once we have a firm consensus on the soft law required for the global business community, then the possibility of evolving into hard law becomes a reality. Whether hard law is better than soft law in the area of CSR is, of course, a matter of great debate and will be part of any future agenda.

Conclusion: the Global Compact as a process to create a sustainable future

The book has traced the evolution of the philosophy of business from a purpose single-mindedly focused on maximizing profit to a purpose described as the creation of sustainable value for all stakeholders. The question then arose as to how to gain a consensus in the global community that this new philosophy is a legitimate one, a fair and just one for all. If the world had a system of global governance, its deliberative bodies would have the opportunity to debate, criticize, offer new proposals and finally legislate new rules of the game (hard law) congruent with the new philosophy of business. Of course, we do not have a world government but we do have the United Nations Global Compact, a set of principles (soft law) that is designed to bring a normative dimension to business practice, specifically in the areas of human rights, labor, the environment and corruption. With over 7,000 businesses in 135 countries and 100 local networks, there is a process underway that holds much promise for the future.

In conclusion, I advocate the United Nations Global Compact as a forum and an instrument to bring the best minds together from business and civil society. There is a growing consensus that with the large aggregates of money and power, multinational corporations have a moral obligation as corporation citizens to assist the poor in the global community, but the extent of these obligations is unclear. The Global Compact offers a forum under the umbrella of the United Nations— with its visibility, global reach, universality, neutrality and convening power—where some of the best members of civil society—NGOs, academic and public policy institutions, individual companies, business associations and labor representatives—can come together to discuss the changing role of business and its *moral* purpose.

Notes

1 For an insightful discussion of Nike's journey to responsible business practices, see Simon Zadek, "The Path to Corporate Responsibility," *Harvard Business Review* 82, no. 12 (2004): 2–10.

2 Brookings Institution researchers estimate that around 70 million people, mostly in China, are lifted out of destitution annually. See Laurence Chandy and Geoffrey Gertz, "Poverty in Numbers: The Changing State of Global Poverty from 2005 to 2015," Policy Brief 2011-01, Global Economy and Development at Brookings, www.brookings.edu.

3 Joseph A. Schumpeter, *Capitalism, Socialism and Democracy* (London: Routledge, 1942).

4 Participants in the Caux Principles have been from 27 countries and include such US companies as 3M International, Chevron, Time, Prudential Insurance Company of America, Procter & Gamble, Chase Manhattan Bank, Medtronic, Monsanto, Honeywell, Cargill, and Bank of America; see www.cauxroundtable.org. For the text of the Caux Principles see *Global Codes of Conduct*, ed. Oliver F. Williams (Notre Dame, Ind.: University of Notre Dame Press 2000), 384–88. For two articles on the Caux Principles, see Gerald F. Cavanagh, "Executives' Code of Business Conduct: Prospects for the Caux Principles," *Global Codes of Conduct*, ed. Williams, 169–82; and Kenneth E. Goodpaster, "The Caux Round Table Principles: Corporate Moral Reflection in a Global Business Environment," *Global Codes of Conduct*, 183–95.

5 Robert Kinlock Massie, "Effective Codes of Conduct: Lessons from the Sullivan and CERES Principles," in *Global Codes of Conduct*, ed. Williams, 287–88.

6 Apparel Industry Partnership's Agreement, 14 April 1997, www.actrav.itcilo.org.

7 For a discussion of the Sullivan Principles, see S. Prakash Sethi and Oliver F. Williams, *Economic Imperatives and Ethical Values in Global Business: The South African Experience and International Codes Today* (Notre Dame, Ind.: University of Notre Dame Press, 2001).

8 See Sean McManus, "The Macbride Principles," December 1997, www1.umn.edu/humanrts/links/macbride.html.

9 One of the best sources for information on the struggle against corruption is the NGO Transparency International: www.transparency.org.

10 Williams, ed., *Global Codes of Conduct*.

11 Kofi Annan, "Business and the UN: A Global Compact of Shared Values and Principles," 31 January 1999, World Economic Forum, Davos, Switzerland; reprinted in *Vital Speeches of the Day* 65, no. 9 (15 February 1999): 260–61. See also Sandrine Tester and Georg Kell, *The United Nations and Business* (New York: St Martin's Press, 2000), 51. Georg Kell is director of the United Nations Global Compact Office.

12 See the UN Global Compact website for extensive discussion on the principles and the list of participants as well as a link to each company's Communication on Progress, www.unglobalcompact.org.

13 For a good sample of the projects companies have undertaken to advance human rights, labor rights, environmental stewardship, and the struggle against corruption, see the *UN Global Compact Annual Review: 2010 Leaders' Summit*, available on the website, www.unglobalcompact.org.

14 Andreas Rasche, Sandra Waddock and Malcolm McIntosh, "The United Nations Global Compact: Retrospect and Prospect," *Business & Society* 52, no. 6 (2012): 6–30.

15 Social Accountability 8000 is a social certification standard designed in 1997 to enable businesses to have decent workplaces based on human rights; see www.sa-intl.org.

16 For the Global Reporting Initiative (GRI), see www.globalreporting.org. The Global Compact suggests that companies use the relevant questions for the COP.

17 ISO 26000 is a guide for a business seeking information on what responsible behavior and action might mean. It is not a set of standards. See www.iso.org/iso/discovering_iso_26000.pdf.

18 Guido Palazzo and Andreas Scherer, "Corporate Legitimacy as Deliberation: A Communicative Framework," *Journal of Business Ethics* 66, no. 1 (2006): 71–88; Lothar Rieth, Melanie Zimmer, Ralph Hamann, and Jon Hanks, "The UN Global Compact in Sub-Saharan Africa: Decentralization and Effectiveness," *Journal of Corporate Citizenship* 7, no. 28 (2007): 99–112.

19 "Global Compact Relaunches China Network," www.unglobalcompact.org/news/172-11-28-2011.

20 The UN Inter-Agency Team consists of UN agencies closely associated with the Global Compact: Office of the UN High Commissioner for Human Rights (OHCHR), International Labour Organization (ILO), UN Environment Programme (UNEP), UN Office on Drugs and Crime (UNODC), UN Development Programme (UNDP), UN Industrial Development Organization (UNIDO), and the UN Entity for Gender Equality and the Empowerment of Women (UN Women).

21 The Government Donor Group as of 2013 consists of: Switzerland, Denmark, Sweden, Spain, Norway, Germany, Finland, France, the United Kingdom, Italy, Colombia, South Korea, and China.

22 See the website of the UN Global Compact Foundation: www.globalcompactfoundation.org.

23 See the website for the Principles for Responsible Investment: www.unpri.org. For a good discussion of the strengths and weaknesses of the PRI, see Catherine Howard and James Gifford, "Are the UN Principles for Responsible Investment Working?" *Ethical Corporation*, November 2008, 30–33.

24 See the website for the PRME: www.unprme.org. See Chapter 2 for the principles and discussion.

25 UN Global Compact, *Annual Review of Business Policies & Actions to Advance Sustainability: 2011 Global Compact Implementation Survey*. See also the *United Nations Global Compact Annual Review 2010*, available at unglobalcompact.org.

26 There are over 3,000 examples of business advancing the MDGs. *Delivering Results: Moving Toward Scale: Accelerating Progress Toward the Millennium Development Goals*, available at unglobalcompact.org.

27 See Bart Slob and Georg Kell, "Debate: UN Global Compact—Is the Compact Raising Corporate Responsibility Standards?" *Ethical Corporation*, 10 May 2008, 1–6; Andreas Rasche, "A Necessary Supplement: What the United Nations Global Compact is and is Not," *Business & Society* 48, no. 4 (2009): 511–37; Robert W. Nason, "Structuring the Global Marketplace: The Impact of the United Nations Global Compact," *Journal of Macromarketing* 24, no. 4 (2008): 418–25; and the blog "Global Compact Critics," globalcompactcritics.blogspot. For a discussion of the UN Global Compact by major international scholars, see *Peace Through Commerce: Responsible Corporate Citizenship and the Ideals of the United Nations Global Compact*, ed. Oliver F. Williams (Notre Dame, Ind.: University of Notre Dame Press, 2008).

28 This paragraph and the next five closely follow an earlier article of mine: "The UN Global Compact: The Challenge and the Promise," *Business Ethics Quarterly* 14, no. 4 (2004): 759–61.

29 Letter to Kofi Annan, Secretary-General, United Nations, 20 July 2000, from Upendra Baxi, Professor of Law, University of Warwick, UK, and former Vice-Chancellor, University of Delhi (India), and others.

30 Letter to Kofi Annan, from Upendra Baxi.

31 Adam Smith, *The Wealth of Nations*, 5th ed., ed. Edwin Cannan (London: Methuen, 1804).

32 Adam Smith, T*he Theory of Moral Sentiments*, 6th ed. (London: A. Millar, 1790).

33 See Patricia H. Werhane, "Business Ethics and the Origins of Contemporary Capitalism: Economics and Ethics in the Work of Adam Smith and Herbert Spencer," *Journal of Business Ethics* 24, no. 3 (2000): 185–98; also Oliver F. Williams, "Catholic Social Teaching: A Communitarian Democratic Capitalism for the New World Order," *Journal of Business Ethics* 12, no. 12 (1993): 919–23. The 1991 encyclical letter of Pope John Paul II, *Centesimus Annus*, makes this central point: "The economy in fact is only one aspect and one dimension of the whole of human activity. If economic life is absolutized, if the production and consumption of goods become the center of social life and society's only value, not subject to any other value, the reason is to be found not so much in the economic system itself as in the fact that the entire socio-cultural system, by ignoring the ethical and religious dimension, has been weakened, and ends by limiting itself to the production of goods and services alone." John Paul II, *Centesimus Annus* (Washington, DC: The US Catholic Conference, 1991), 77.

34 Sandrine Tester and Georg Kell, *The United Nations and Business* (New York: St Martin's Press, 2000), 51.

35 S. Prakash Sethi, "Global Compact is Another Exercise in Futility," *The Financial Express*, 8 September 2003. For a comprehensive discussion of codes of conduct, see S. Prakash Sethi, *Setting Global Standards: Guidelines for Creating Codes of Conduct in Multinational Corporations* (New York: John Wiley & Sons, 2003).

36 Slob and Kell, "Debate: UN Global Compact," 1–6.

37 Lynn Sharp Paine, *Value Shift: Why Companies Must Merge Social and Financial Imperatives to Achieve Superior Performance* (New York: McGraw-Hill, 2003), 20–23.

38 See the list of participants on the Global Compact website, www.unglobalc ompact.org.

39 Georg Kell, "12 Years Later: Reflections on the Growth of the UN Global Compact," *Business & Society* 53, no. 31 (2012): 31–52.

40 Kell, "12 Years Later," 36.

41 For an excellent discussion, see Minhee Yang, "The Evolution, Transmission and Hardening of Soft Laws in Corporate Social Responsibility: Focusing on Northeast Asian Region (China, Japan, and Korea)," thesis for Master's degree in International Relations at the Graduate Institute of Peace Studies, Kyung Hee University, South Korea, August 2012. To obtain, contact minhee612@gmail.com. See also Chip Pitts, Michael Kerr and Richard Janda, *Corporate Social Responsibility: A Legal Analysis* (LexisNexis Canada, 2009).

5 Conclusion

Moving from incremental progress
toward transformational action
in shaping an inclusive and
sustainable economy

- **Companies advancing an inclusive and sustainable society**
- **Homeplus: South Korea's top-tier hypermarket chain**
- **Merck & Co. Inc.: true to its founder**
- **Conclusion: where have we been and where are we going?**

One of the reasons why consumers expect so much of business today is because it has been so successful. Business has been hugely successful in producing goods and services that consumers want and, hence, it has accrued vast economic power. Large businesses, because of their success, dominate our world. For example, in recent years General Electric (GE) had sales of over US$140 billion a year and had over 300,000 employees; IBM had sales of over $100 billion and some 430,000 employees. Of the over 190 nations in the world, very few have government revenues that approach large multinational business revenues. Many argue that business, with its wide array of resources, especially management skills, is uniquely positioned to solve some of the problems of the wider society. Many companies argue that corporate social responsibility (CSR), corporate citizenship, or whichever term they choose to use, is in the interest of business but that participation in these projects is not based solely on a traditional business case. In a 2008 special report in the *Economist*, several business leaders are quoted.[1] Ed Potter of Coca-Cola speaks of a "broad philosophical commitment to sustainable communities." Edward Bickham of Anglo American suggests that "sustainability is a threshold requirement with any competitive gain staying at the margins." Dr Gail Kendall of CLP Group speaks of the retrofitting of power stations to reduce emissions as nothing to do with competition in the market: "It is our shareholders and regulators expectations that this is a correct thing to do in the community ... We see it as the right thing to do." Jeffrey Immelt, CEO of GE, in discussing some of the company's projects throughout the world, commented: "The reason people come to work for GE is that they want to be about something that is bigger than themselves. People want to work hard, they want to get promoted, and they want stock options. But they also want to work for a company that makes a difference, a company that's doing great things in the world."[2] Enabling community and building a sustainable and inclusive economy in the world are goals that flow from the identity and culture of a business; they are intrinsic objectives.

What we are experiencing is that under the influence of the wider society, there is a broadening of the values of many business people and, hence, a broadening of the values of capitalism; the very purpose of business has moved from making money to creating sustainable value for all stakeholders. To be sure, this phenomenon is not present in all business, but a growing number of business people want to make a difference. They are asking about ultimate purpose, about what most deeply matters in life, and they want to chart a life plan that draws on the full range of resources of the human spirit. This new focus is what many describe as a focus on spiritual values. From this standpoint, sustainability reflects the connectedness of business with the wider society. Business must not only take responsibility for its own activities, but also for some of the problems in the wider society. This wider vision of companies, the belief that doing well and doing good are not opposites, is championed by many management scholars. Jerry Porras and James Collins in *Built to Last* discuss a number of these "visionary companies."[3] For example, Merck Pharmaceutical Company has a mission statement which includes that the company "devotes extensive efforts to increase access to medicines through far-reaching programs that not only donate Merck medicines, but help deliver them to the people who need them." Merck's employees feel good about their company and this has reportedly enhanced productivity and decreased turnover of employees.[4]

What the world needs now is many more Mercks, companies that have a wider vision of the role of business in society. As discussed in Chapter 4, the United Nations Global Compact (UNGC), as of 2013, had over 7,000 signatories from business based in more than 140 countries. These companies employ more than 50 million people representing all industries, all ranges of wealth on the part of home countries and all sizes of companies. To achieve the transformation envisioned to an inclusive and sustainable global society, however, it will take many more companies. Today there are over 80,000 multinational companies and to garner a critical mass of these businesses, all working toward a common goal, it will take renewed effort. The UNGC has set a target of 20,000 companies by 2020 to have the critical mass to advance significantly the sustainable vision.[5] At the same time, there will be great effort applied to ensure that signatories actually advance the sustainable vision through their strategic plans and projects. This will be a qualitative effort as well as a quantitative one.[6]

Companies advancing an inclusive and sustainable society

While there are thousands of companies in the Global Compact that are models of sustainability and inclusivity, it may be helpful to discuss two companies to give the reader an idea of how the conceptual foundations bear fruit in an actual enterprise. Porras and Collins suggest that to understand a company, one should focus on its vision, values and purpose.[7] The purpose is "like a guiding star on the horizon—forever pursued but never reached," the most fundamental reason for existing. The values of a firm are those characteristics that define who you are; you couldn't live without them. The vision is what focuses attention on a specific goal that energizes employees because it "is bold, exciting and emotionally charged." For example, Southwest Airlines, a highly admired and economically successful company, says its purpose is to "democratize the skies, to give more people the freedom to fly." The company wanted to price airline travel so that people who would normally take a train or bus could fly. The company's vision was to have a world where everyone has the ability to fly and to live a full life. Its core values are freedom, enhancing the quality of life and creating a human workplace. The company's mission, the way they planned to realize the vision, was to run the company so that there would be low fares and high employee morale.[8] It may be helpful to focus on two Global Compact companies that embrace much of what is discussed in this volume, that is, that the purpose of business is to create sustainable value for all stakeholders. These companies see CSR as their contribution to sustainable development.

Homeplus: South Korea's top-tier hypermarket chain[9]

Founded in 1999 with two hypermarket (supermarket) stores, as of 2013 the company had 134 superstores across Korea with sales of over 11.5 trillion won (about $10 billion). During the first 10 years the company averaged 50 percent growth and profits increased 150 percent each year. With over 26,000 employees, the Korean retailer has been recognized by the Korean Management Association Consulting (KMAC), as Korea's Most Admired Company in 2011. (KMAC's rating is Korea's equivalent of *Fortune*'s most admired companies.)

For purposes of this study, the significant feature of Homeplus is that it has always integrated social/environmental and financial values. As the KMAC Director Lee Lib said, "In fact Homeplus incorporated CSR in its management. It is an integral part of Homeplus' way of doing business. In this sense, Homeplus created the concept of CSR management." The chairman and CEO from its founding in 1999 until 2013, Seung-han Lee, always believed that a business is intertwined with its surroundings; for the company to be healthy, the surroundings must be healthy. This conviction influenced a wide range of decisions.

The purpose of Homeplus is captured in the company mantra: "We make what matters better, together." Its three core values are: "No one tries harder for customers;" "Treat people how we would like to be treated;" and "We use our scale for good." Bringing together the purpose and values of the company, the firm spells out what this means for customers, colleagues and communities. For customers, the company strives to provide "everything they need, made better and easier; outstanding value for everyone; advice, inspiration and a smile; an easy, seamless, personalized experience; and a thank you." All this is designed "to help them to get the most out of life." For colleagues, the purpose and values mean "being proud of what we do; creating a great place to work: happy, honest and inspiring; providing opportunities for us all to be our best; building relationships based on shared values and respect, a place where we all contribute, make a difference and can be ourselves." All this is designed "to help us get the most out of work." For communities, using its scale for good, the company strives to create "new opportunities for young people, wherever we are in the world; to reverse the trend in obesity, in all our markets; and to lead the industry in cutting our food waste." All this is designed "to help leave the World a better place."

From the perspective of this study, the most striking feature of Homeplus is that from the start of the company there were two equal and parallel logics operative, a financial logic and a social logic. S.H. Lee, not too unlike leaders discussed earlier in this volume, certainly believed that the company had to return well on investment but, at the same time, he held that the purpose of the company included advancing societal objectives and to some extent helping to provide a meaningful life for stakeholders. Well before it was fashionable, and before we had the concepts to describe it, he saw that the purpose of business was to create sustainable value for stakeholders.

S.H. Lee's vision was that the superstores should have "high-quality, get-what-you-pay-for-products," but at the same time that they should be community centers. On the ground floor of the stores you could find clinics, restaurants, playgrounds, cultural centers as well as educational facilities. Lee began his professional life in the Samsung Group in 1970 and only in 1999, when Samsung started Homeplus in a joint venture with the large UK retailer TESCO, did he have a top leadership post. Critics of Lee's philosophy of management were not hard to find. Was Lee sure that his community center notion for Homeplus stores would help the company beat the competition in selling products? Of course not. He was convinced, however, that it was the right thing to do. Pleasing customers and the surrounding community would in the short run create sustainable value for those stakeholders and he hoped that this would create value for the shareholders in the long run. As it turned out, he was correct. In record time, Homeplus became the number-two discount chain in Korea and was on firm financial ground. "CSR is no longer a peripheral issue. It is now one of the major purposes of companies ... In the past, the primary goal of firms was to gain profits. Now, they also have to consider how to make the world a better place to live in by including CSR among their core values." A key responsibility of corporate management is to provide a "consistent and balanced management of company performance targets." Unlike many of his competitors, however, performance targets are wide ranging: customer, operation, finance, people, and community.

The company has numerous activities that demonstrate that it believes in corporate citizenship or corporate social responsibility. While there is no attempt to discuss all the CSR projects here, several are highlighted to give a flavor of the corporate philosophy in this regard. Focusing on four areas, what the company calls "four loves," the projects fall under one of the categories: environment, sharing, neighbor, and family.

Environment

Homeplus takes very seriously the threat of global warming and climate change and has used its considerable influence to persuade its employees, customers, and all Korean society to participate in programs designed to save energy, recycle, and reduce CO_2 emissions.

The company itself has adopted a Green Management plan which includes having environmentally friendly stores that reduce carbon emissions by 50 percent and energy by 40 percent. Utilizing measures to increase transportation efficiency and reduce CO_2 emissions related to its distribution network, Homeplus has lowered its carbon footprint by 50 percent in several years.

Homeplus has organized activities to educate children about environmental issues. With the UN Environment Programme, the company sponsors an annual painting contest which draws over 45,000 children as participants. The company also runs a Green Leaders Program, educating more than 7,000 children about crucial environmental matters. The plan is to increase that number to 100,000 by 2020.

Another innovative environmental feature is the recently constructed training facility which is the first of its kind as a carbon-zero modern building. Called the TESCO-Homeplus Academy, the state-of-the-art facility will serve 14 countries of the TESCO Group with its 22 lecture rooms and 87 dormitory rooms. Each year over 24,000 students will come to Korea and learn not only how to serve customers more effectively but also how to preserve and promote the physical environment.

Neighbor

One of the key CSR activities involves outreach to the poor and least advantaged with cultural education and to others in the community with a wide variety of lifelong educational opportunities. Homeplus has 118 Schools of Extended Education, with 6,800 instructors teaching over 400 courses to upwards of 1 million students a year. In selecting a new store location, the company often searches to find places where there is a lack of cultural and educational opportunities so that Homeplus might provide those services.

The company also supports over 100 welfare centers that take care of poor children, including offering some educational courses.

Family

Homeplus has programs to address the national problem of low birth rates in Korea. Striving to create "a childbirth-friendly social environment," the company partnered with the YMCA to create courses for professional nannies. These programs not only educate people to care for infants but also create jobs for women.

The company also has programs for women who left the workforce to raise a family and now want to return to a career. Over 60 stores have "Employment Assistance Service Centers" staffed by the Ministry of Gender Equality and Family to assist women who want to return to employment.

In sports, the company operates a Youth Football Club both to develop Korean football and to teach young boys the qualities of character that enable a good life. A relatively new program, the students learn environmental and social values as well as leadership skills.

The Work & Family Balance Campaign is a company initiative to assist employees in developing a healthy work-life and family-life balance.

In 2010, 81.5 percent of the employees were satisfied with the work and family balance according to the annual employee viewpoint survey.

Sharing

The Save Young Lives Campaign is funded by Homeplus, some 264 of its suppliers, and over 28 million customers who bought products knowing that a percentage of the cost was going to the campaign. The fund supports poor children with terminal diseases such as cancer and leukemia and assists financing young people who are in foster care.

Under the rubric of sharing, Homeplus implements policies and programs that ensure that the dual objectives of sustainable growth and social contribution are equally advanced. Social contributions include such things as charity fund raisers, staff and customer volunteer programs, and education for children on the value of sharing. On the business side, there is considerable effort put forth to enhance partnerships with suppliers so that they might participate in sustainable growth. The 2010/11 Sustainability Report details these efforts.

The charity fundraisers, called Homeplus charity bazaars, sell goods donated by suppliers, customers and staff. About 100 of these fundraisers are held each year with over 700 Homeplus staff volunteers. The proceeds are given to families and children in poverty. Staff participate in a number of other activities for the needs of the poor, donating upwards of 57,000 volunteer hours a year.

One unique feature of Homeplus is its CSR research center. Established in 1999, the R&D center explores new issues with the assumption that CSR is an investment and not simply a cost. For example, the center has advanced a program to advise suppliers on CSR initiatives. While suppliers might not have the resources to launch CSR programs on their own, with the center's knowledge and capability they can move ahead with meaningful social programs.

Not surprisingly, Homeplus' Communication on Progress (COP) qualifies for the Global Compact Advanced Level, indicating that the company meets a higher standard of corporate sustainability performance and disclosure. Details of the criteria for the GC Advanced Level are spelled out on the Global Compact website.[10]

In my view, one of the key reasons for the great success of Homeplus is S.H. Lee's intuitive understanding that to engage people you must address not only the head but also the heart, the rational as well as the affective dimension of the person. All the stakeholders are addressed in this fashion; there is an emotional connection. Several examples may be helpful. In 2009, the company formed the "eParan Foundation" which oversees all the CSR activities under the rubric of the "four loves." What is eParan? It is a CSR character known and loved throughout Korea. It has rabbit-like ears shaped like a leaf, the face of a cute puppy, the body of a friendly bear, four-finger hands similar to those of a koala, and the feet of a brave lion with the courage to protect the natural environment. You can find eParan, dressed in his green outfit, roaming in the stores of Homeplus, always bringing a smile to young and old alike. He also brings the environmental vision of Homeplus to the heart. We are told that "e" "stands for environmental, ethical, extended education, exciting, e-world and everlasting." "Paran" refers to the green campaign to promote and protect the environment.

Another image used often is the "Great Stone Face." S.H. Lee tells us that in his youth the novel of that name by Nathaniel Hawthorne had an important influence on him. Just as the Great Stone Face was loved and respected far and wide in the novel, Lee's vision is that companies should behave so that they are loved and respected. The Stone Face has two dimensions, the head and the heart, reflecting the two dimensions of business: economic development and social progress. Both dimensions are essential for the creation of a better world, according to Homeplus. Employing this image, the company hopes stakeholders form a unique bond with Homeplus.

Another important role of S.H. Lee is that since 2010 he served as the president of UN Global Compact Korea Local Network, a coalition of over 230 businesses and other groups that are committed to advancing the 10 principles of the compact as well as broader UN goals. Under Lee's leadership, the UN Global Compact Korea Network has become one of the best in the world, with large companies taking on major projects in the global community. For example, the Hyundai Motor Group has developed a technical training center to educate young people for employment in Ghana, and started children's centers in Cambodia and Equatorial Guinea. LG Electronics has initiated community projects for development in Ethiopia, Bangladesh and Cambodia. POSCO has formed training institutes in Africa to enhance agricultural production, and developed children's educational centers in Zimbabwe and Mozambique. The KT Corporation has established an elementary school and a wireless IT system in Rwanda. SK Telecom has supported plastic surgery for children with facial deformities in Vietnam. Kia Motors has supported tree planting in Mali to prevent soil erosion. Yuhan Kimberly has restored forests in North Korea and Mongolia. The Korea Water Resource Corporation has developed programs to solve water problems in Cambodia, Laos, Mongolia, the Philippines and Vietnam. Additional examples are available on the website of the UN Global Compact Korea Local Network.[11]

After 14 years of leading the company, S.H. Lee announced in February 2013 that he would step down as CEO but would remain as Homeplus Group chairman and retain the chairmanship of the e-Paran Foundation, Homeplus' corporate social responsibility arm.

What is clear is that if all business leaders were to take sustainable development as seriously as Lee, the world would be a much better place. What follows is a discussion of another company demonstrating leadership in sustainable development.

Merck & Co. Inc.: true to its founder[12]

Founded in 1891, Merck today has operations in more than 140 countries, sales of over $48 billion and over 50,000 employees. One of the seven largest pharmaceutical companies in the world, its annual CSR contributions are about $1 billion a year in cash and product. Merck is not known for writing checks, however, but for applying its scientific and managerial talent to improving global health.

Similar to Homeplus, Merck has always operated with a dual logic, financial and social. This philosophy of business was expressed in 1950 by George Merck, then CEO: "We try to remember that medicine is for the patient. We try never to forget that medicine is for the people. It is not for the profits. The profits follow, and if we have remembered that, they have never failed to appear." Son of the founder, George Merck has influenced the purpose, values and vision of the company to this day.

The core values of the company are four: preserving and improving human life; promoting the highest standards of ethics and integrity; expanding access to their products; and employing a diverse workforce that values collaboration. The mission of the company is "to promote innovative, distinctive products and services that save and improve lives, satisfy customer needs and to be recognized as a great place to work."

There is no attempt to detail all the CSR projects of Merck but rather the chapter focuses on two projects that illustrate clearly how Merck understands the purpose of business: to create sustainable value for all stakeholders. The river blindness case as well as the HIV/AIDS in Botswana case demonstrate that when the company had difficult decisions to make it employed a financial logic as well as a social logic and, in these cases, the social logic triumphed or overrode the financial logics.

The river blindness case[13]

As you enter the spacious lobby of Merck's corporate headquarters in Whitehouse Station, New Jersey, you are struck by a large, life-size bronze statue of a young boy leading an elderly man, each holding on to a stick to keep the two together. Titled "The Gift of Sight," this statue is a reminder to Merck employees as they come to work each day that river blindness had deprived 60 percent of the residents of some West African villages of sight, causing blindness for over 270,000 people and impaired vision for upwards of 500,000 in tropical regions of Africa and Latin America. Merck had found a cure and made that cure accessible to all. This is a great source of pride to the employees. No longer does the man need to be led.

As the story goes, in 1980 Merck had a very popular and effective medicine that killed harmful parasites in cattle. Scientists at Merck were convinced that this drug, if modified, could be a cure for river blindness (onchocerciasis), caused by similar parasites in humans who were bitten by the black fly. To develop a drug for human consumption and have it tested in clinical studies required by the US government could cost upwards of $100 million. The problem here was that there was little prospect for Merck to recoup its investment because the people who were likely targets of the black fly were very poor, living in countries that had little funding for public health. The question was: should Merck make an investment in a drug that had no chance of earning any return for shareholders?

For Merck, the answer was easier than it might have been for most companies, for the firm was way ahead of the curve in understanding that the purpose of business was not only increasing the financial bottom line but also building civil society. In this case, they opted for social purpose knowing that there would be no enhancement of the financial bottom line. The right to see, which the new drug would secure, overrode making money. After seven years of research, the company was successful and in 1987 Merck started distributing the new drug called Mectizan to "all that need it for as long as needed."[14] As of today, over 2 billion tablets have been distributed. With a partnership with the World Bank, Merck makes the drug available in 30 African countries, six Latin American countries and Yemen.

Botswana's African Comprehensive HIV/AIDS Partnerships (ACHAP)[15]

In 1999, the HIV/AIDS pandemic was a frightening prospect to many scientists. It was estimated that 34 million people were living with the disease throughout the world. In sub-Saharan Africa where there was extreme poverty and little access to medical care and treatment, some 23 million people had HIV/AIDS. Infection rates in Zimbabwe were estimated at 25 percent and in Botswana 36 percent. There is no cure for the disease but there are very helpful drugs (antiretrovirals, or ARVs) which treat the symptoms and allow people to live a relatively normal life. A small number of research pharmaceutical firms had developed various ARV medicines and they were under increasing pressure from some nongovernmental organizations (NGOs) to give the drug for free to all those who could not afford it. Given the number of people infected, the fact that the medicines had to be taken for life, and the fact that the medicines required careful monitoring of the patient, giving it away to all was out of the question in the judgment of most scientists. What then was the moral responsibility of a company like Merck which has always tried to be socially responsible?

While Merck realized it would be impossible to solve the whole HIV/AIDS problem in sub-Saharan Africa, it believed it must do something to contribute to its solution in the spirit of the founder's vision, values and mission. After careful deliberation and consultation with many possible partners, Merck joined with the Bill and Melinda Gates Foundation and together they sought one country where they might provide care and treatment for those suffering from HIV/AIDS. From Merck's experience with other projects providing access to medicines, for example the river blindness project, the company knew that donating medicines was not enough; they would have to improve the health care infrastructure as well as provide training for the medical workers involved. Involving the government of the country selected was also essential.

The scientists pointed out that the country selected had to be politically stable with little threat of civil war, as a patient on ARVs could not have the medicine schedule interrupted. Others noted that it was crucial to have the full support of the government leaders as well as the local people. Finally, after much analysis, on 10 July 2000 the announcement was made. Officials from the Republic of Botswana, the Gates Foundation and Merck announced that they were forming a partnership to improve the overall state of HIV/AIDS care and treatment in Botswana. Called the African Comprehensive HIV/AIDS Partnership (ACHAP), the program was initially funded with a grant of $50 million from the Gates Foundation and $50 million from Merck. Merck also provided two antiretroviral medicines for ACHAP as well as for the government's other AIDS program. At the time of the establishment of ACHAP, only 5 percent of the people with AIDS were receiving treatment; in 2013 that number is 90 percent or more. It is estimated that over 50,000 lives have been saved because of ACHAP.

For purposes of this study, it is important to note that the Botswana program was an integral part of strategy for the company and not a separate initiative under the CSR label. Integrating social issues in strategic planning is part of the DNA of Merck and in full accord with its mission, core values and vision. The responsibility for the program was given to Merck's head of Europe, the Middle East and Africa, and those involved were seeking to learn how to bring drugs to poor countries at an affordable cost.

In August 2010, Merck and Gates announced that they were each giving an additional $30 million to fund the final phase of the program until 2015. In this second phase of the program, 137,000 people currently on antiretrovirals will continue, prevention of the disease will be a focus, and local leaders will take over the operation. ACHAP has assisted in creating 32 ARV treatment sites and 170 clinics in Botswana, and hopes to have zero new infections by 2016.

While there is certainly no claim that Merck or any other company is a perfect company without stain or blemish,[16] it is a good example of a company that believes that the purpose of business is to create sustainable value for all stakeholders and that some things must be done because they are the right things to do, even if no immediate benefit to the company is apparent. If every company of Merck's size were to take on such projects, sustainable development for the planet would be within reach.

Conclusion: where have we been and where are we going?

The book has traced the evolution of the term CSR from meaning corporate philanthropy administered by a special unit in the company to all those activities that advance sustainable development and are incorporated into the strategic plan of the business. Following the Brundtland Commission definition, sustainable development is understood as that which "meets the needs of the present without compromising the ability of future generations to meet their own needs." Originally the term referred to protecting natural resources so that the physical environment was healthy. Gradually it became clear that just as business relies on the physical environment for its long-term health, it also relies on social structures, an ethical climate, good governance and stakeholder relationships for its success.

The book discussed how some companies opposed the expansion of the role of business in society, focusing in some detail on how business was very reluctant to get involved with the apartheid struggle, even when it was complicit in denying human rights to blacks. There were other companies, however, which had leaders who understood that they were in the midst of a paradigm shift, that the very purpose of business was developing, and that business should at the very least respect human rights and perhaps even protect and advance them.

Due to a host of factors including the threat of climate change and our expanding carbon footprint, the globalization of the economy, and the realization that dire poverty is a reality for almost a billion people, more and more companies are volunteering to do their part in advancing sustainable development. In this volume the term CSR is used to refer to the contribution of business to advancing sustainable development.

What has become clear is that there is a need to have a central organization which can be a forum to gain consensus on the norms and values for sustainable development in the global economy. The book makes the case that the United Nations Global Compact is the best organization for this important role. This final chapter highlights two UNGC member companies involved in serious projects advancing sustainable development. The point is not that these are perfect companies but rather that if a critical mass of companies took on projects of the same scope, the journey toward sustainable development would be well on its way.

The final point is a reminder that if we are to move toward genuine sustainable development, everyone must get involved. Many consumers must be educated—as some companies have realized. Governments must examine subsidies that are counterproductive as well as consider creating a stable price for carbon. NGOs must work harder to apply pressure for change. Academic institutions must highlight the whole range of sustainability issues in their programs as outlined in the Principles for Responsible Management Education. Investors must increasingly factor environmental, social/ethical and governance issues in investment decisions as the Principles for Responsible Investment (PRI) encourage.[17] Large companies must assist their suppliers in moving toward sustainable business. The list goes on.

Sustainable development and the business contribution, CSR, is a challenge but also a promise. If we want a better world, we cannot do without it.

Notes

1 Paul Kielstra, "Doing Good: Business and the Sustainability Challenge," *Economist Intelligence Report*, February 2008, 38.
2 Marc Gunther, "Money and Morals at GE," *Fortune*, 1 November 2004, 1.
3 Jerry Porras and James Collins, *Built to Last: Successful Habits of Visionary Companies* (New York: HarperCollins, 1994).
4 Man on a Mission, Merck's (MRK) Mission Statement.

5 UN Global Compact, "UN Global Compact Strategy 2014–16," 11 March 2013 (Draft for Consultation).
6 As of April 2013, 4,135 participants had been expelled from the Global Compact because of not submitting a Communication on Progress; see unglobalcompact.org.
7 Porras and Collins, *Built to Last*.
8 For a discussion of Southwest Airlines, see Oliver Williams, "Is it Possible to Have a Business Based on Solidarity and Mutual Trust? The Challenge of Catholic Social Teaching to Capitalism and the Promise of Southwest Airlines," *Journal of Catholic Social Thought* 9, no. 1 (2012): 59–69.
9 All the information on Homeplus came from a 90-minute interview with the Chairman and CEO Seung-han Lee (S.H. Lee) on Friday 29 March 2013, as well as written documents. The major written document is the company's Communication on Progress for the UN Global Compact, *Homeplus Sustainability Report 2010/11*. In addition, see Kim Tae-gyu, "Paradigm Shift: New Movement in CSR, Homeplus Chairman Lee Seung-han Declares CSR is an End in Itself," *The Korea Times*, 28 January 2013.
10 UN Global Compact, "Differentiation Programme," www.unglobalcompact.org/COP/differentiation_programme.html.
11 UN Global Compact, "Global Compact Network Korea," www.unglobalcompact.Kr/eng.
12 The information on Merck comes from the COP, UN Global Compact, *Merck Corporate Responsibility Report 2011*, as well as several other sources. See also Merck's homepage: www.merck.com.
13 Information for this section was obtained from several sources: "FACT Sheet—Merck Mectizan Donation Program—River Blindness (Onchocerciasis)," www.merck.com/cr/docs/River%20Blindness%20Fact%20Sheet.pdf; and Jung Joo Hwang, "Is Merck's Corporate Social Responsibility Good for Global Health?" 26 March 2012, irps.ucsd.edu/assets/001/503692.pdf.
14 "Fact Sheet—Merck Mectizan Donation Program—River Blindness (Onchocerciasis)."
15 Information for this section was obtained from several sources: Themba Moeti, Innocent Chingombe and Godfrey Musuka, "Public Private Partnership and Development—Progress Towards Achieving the Millennium Development Goals Through an Effective HIV/AIDS Response: The ACHAP Experience in Botswana," *Sustainable Development*, ed. Oliver F. Williams (Notre Dame, Ind.: University of Notre Dame Press, 2013), 74–119; Ilavenil Ramiah and Michael R. Reich, "Building Effective Public-Private Partnerships: Experiences and Lessons from the African Comprehensive HIV/AIDS Partnerships (ACHAP)," *Social Science and Medicine* 63, no. 2 (2006): 397–408; and Merck news release, "Merck Provides New Funding to Fight HIV/AIDS in Botswana," 24 August 2010.
16 Merck has not been without it critics. For example, see the ongoing discussion of Vioxx in the *Lancet*: Peter Juni, Stephan Reichenbach, Paul A. Dieppe and Matthias Egger, "Discontinuation of Vioxx," 2005.
17 Members of the PRI sent a letter to 1,900 companies in 44 countries on 27 March 2013, encouraging those companies to join the UN Global Compact. The companies are all included in the FTSE All World Index, www.unglobalcompact.org/news/312-03-27-2013.

Select bibliography

Thomas Donaldson, *The Ethics of International Business* (Oxford: Oxford University Press, 1989). Authored by a major scholar in the field, this book, although it limits the human rights responsibilities of business, is a pioneer in the discussion.

William C. Frederick, *Corporations Be Good! The Story of Corporate Social Responsibility* (Indianapolis, Ind.: Dog Ear Publishing, 2006). This is a very readable account by a scholar who has followed the issues closely of how the business world has come to accept and promote corporate social responsibility.

Kenneth E. Goodpaster, *Conscience and Corporate Culture* (Malden, Mass.: Blackwell Publishing, 2007). Authored by a philosopher, the book focuses on the developed conscience of the business leader to ground the advancement of human welfare in the world of commerce.

Bradley K. Googins, Philip H. Mirvis, and Steven A. Rochlin, *Beyond Good Company: Next Generation Corporate Citizenship* (New York: Palgrave Macmillan, 2007). An insightful book by a political scientist, an organizational psychologist and a social policy expert which argues that the purpose of business should be transformed from economic gain to creating value, and not just monetary value.

John W. Houck and Oliver F. Williams, eds., *Is the Good Corporation Dead? Social Responsibility in a Global Economy* (Lanham, Md.: Rowman & Littlefield Publishers, 1996). Authored by scholars and practitioners, the book includes essays by Richard T. DeGeorge, Ronald M. Green, James E. Post, S. Prakash Sethi, Lee A. Tavis, Michael Novak, and Oliver F. Williams. Chapters on Motorola, Hershey Foods, and Chevron are included.

Wayne Visser, *Landmarks for Sustainability: Events and Initiatives that have Changed Our World* (Sheffield: Greenleaf Publishing, 2009). The book charts the expansion of the sustainability movement from a marginal status to mainstream thinking, from concern for the physical environment to all that has been known as corporate social responsibility and corporate citizenship.

David Vogel, *The Market for Virtue: The Potential and Limits of Corporate Social Responsibility* (Washington, DC: Brookings Institution Press, 2005). Authored by an important scholar, the central thesis of the book is that

"CSR is best understood as a niche rather than a generic strategy: it makes business sense for some firms in some areas under some circumstances."

Sandra Waddock and Malcolm McIntosh, *SEE Change: Making the Transition to a Sustainable Enterprise Economy* (Sheffield: Greenleaf Publishing, 2011). The book argues for a serious rethinking of capitalism, a focus that sees that "social, human, and environmental benefits [are] as important as making a profit."

Oliver F. Williams, ed., *Peace Through Commerce: Responsible Corporate Citizenship and the Ideals of the United Nations Global Compact* (Notre Dame, Ind.: University of Notre Dame Press, 2008). Authored by business scholars and practitioners, the chapters focus on how corporate power and management skills can be marshaled through the UN Global Compact to advance justice and peace in the developing world.

Index

3M 18, 90

Abrams, Frank W. 7–8, 43, 46, 55
accountability 36; legitimacy 32;
  monitoring 75–76; NGO 85, 86;
  Social Accountability 8000 79, 90;
  UNGC 83, 85
ACHAP (African Comprehensive
  HIV/AIDS Partnership) 102–4
ACOA (American Committee on
  Africa) 11–12, 16, 23; Houser,
  George 11–12, 16
activist movement 10, 14, 16, 17, 19,
  22, 24, 86
Alford, Helen 39
AMCHAM (American Chamber of
  Commerce) 21
Amnesty International 25, 86
Anglo American 93
Annan, Kofi 86; UNGC 44, 72, 76,
  77, 79–80, 87; *see also* UNGC
anti-apartheid struggle, role of
  business 2, 5, 11–24, 31–33, 35,
  55, 73, 104; ACOA 11–12, 16, 23;
  activist movement 10, 14, 16, 17,
  19, 22, 24; apartheid laws 11, 15,
  21, 22; Arthur D. Little, Inc. 19,
  21; Biko, Steve 23; bridging 15;
  church groups 12–13, 20, 23, 24;
  civil and political rights 12, 15, 16,
  17, 18, 21, 23, 31; disinvestment
  11–12, 16, 19, 20, 21, 23–24;
  education and training 20, 21–22;
  license to operate 32; human
  rights 11, 14, 15, 24, 31; moral
  obligation toward justice 14–15,

24, 32; NAACP 11; NGO 31;
  paradigm shift 11–24, 73 (business
  as part of the problem 12–19;
  integrating economic and social
  values 19–24); SACC 20; selective
  purchasing ordinance 33;
  shareholder resolution campaign
  13, 19, 22; Tutu, Desmond 19, 21
  (Tutu 'Principles' 20); US, 1986
  Comprehensive Anti-Apartheid
  Act 23; *see also* ICCR; Sullivan,
  Leon
Apple 63, 65

Ban Ki-moon 72, 87
Bowen, Harold Rothman 6–7; *Social
  Responsibilities of the Businessman*
  3, 6, 46
business 1; business ethics 5, 25, 26,
  46; Donaldson, Thomas 26;
  human rights 26, 56–64, 77, 105;
  success and economic power 93;
  sustainability 104; values 46; *see
  also entries below for* business
business ecology model 10–11, 54,
  68; market capitalism/business
  ecology model paradigm shift
  10–11, 13, 22, 46, 47; Steiner,
  George 10–11; *see also* market
  capitalism model
business leaders 7, 38, 93; business,
  purpose of 31, 38–39, 40–44, 47,
  104–5; Caux Principles 75, 76;
  education of 8, 45, 46; global
  ethics 75; sustainable development
  93, 101; trust 35

Routledge Global Institutions Series

'

Millennium Development Goals (MDGs)
For a people-centered development agenda?
by Sakiko Fukuda-Parr (The New School)

UNICEF
by Richard Jolly (University of Sussex)

The Bank for International Settlements
The politics of global financial supervision in the age
of high finance
by Kevin Ozgercin (SUNY College at Old Westbury)

International Migration
by Khalid Koser (Geneva Centre for Security Policy)

Human Development
by Richard Ponzio

The International Monetary Fund (2nd edition)
Politics of conditional lending
by James Raymond Vreeland (Georgetown University)

The UN Global Compact
by Catia Gregoratti (Lund University)

Institutions for Women's Rights
*by Charlotte Patton (York College, CUNY) and
Carolyn Stephenson (University of Hawaii)*

International Aid
by Paul Mosley (University of Sheffield)

Global Consumer Policy
by Karsten Ronit (University of Copenhagen)

The Changing Political Map of Global Governance
*by Anthony Payne (University of Sheffield) and
Stephen Robert Buzdugan (Manchester Metropolitan University)*

Coping with Nuclear Weapons
by W. Pal Sidhu

Post-2015 UN Development
Making change happen
edited by Stephen Browne (FUNDS Project) and
Thomas G. Weiss (The CUNY Graduate Center)

Who Participates?
States, bureaucracies, NGOs and global governance
by Molly Ann Ruhlman

The United Nations as a Knowledge Organization
by Nanette Svenson (Tulane University)

United Nations Centre on Transnational Corporations (UNCTC)
by Khalil Hamdani and Lorraine Ruffing

The International Criminal Court
The Politics and practice of prosecuting atrocity crimes
by Martin Mennecke (University of Copenhagen)

For further information regarding the series, please contact:
Craig Fowlie, Publisher, Politics & International Studies
Taylor & Francis
2 Park Square, Milton Park, Abingdon
Oxford OX14 4RN, UK
+44 (0)207 842 2057 Tel
+44 (0)207 842 2302 Fax
Craig.Fowlie@tandf.co.uk
www.routledge.com

Printed in the USA/Agawam, MA
April 29, 2014